Building a Caring, Cooperative Classroom

A Social Skills Primer

James Bellanca

Skylight Publishing
Palatine, Illinois

Building a Caring, Cooperative Classroom:
A Social Skills Primer
First Printing

Published by Skylight Publishing, Inc.
200 E. Wood Street, Suite 250
Palatine, Illinois 60067
800-348-4474 (in northern Illinois 708-991-6300)
FAX 708-991-6420

Editing: Julia E. Noblitt, Robin Fogarty
Book Design: Bruce Leckie
Illustration: David Stockman
Type Composition: Donna Ramirez
Production Coordination: Ari Ohlson

Printed in the United States of America

Library of Congress Catalog Card Number: 91-62547

ISBN 0-932935-35-4

CONTENTS

Building A Caring, Cooperative Classroom

"A cooperative classroom? Students who respect and care for each other? My students only know how to put each other down."

"Teach students how to cooperate? Are you kidding? I don't have time to do everything else as it is. I've got test scores to raise."

"Social skills? Aren't they the job of the parents?"

"Come on now. You have to be kidding. What else do you want to add to the curriculum. Isn't it already an overstuffed sausage?"

"Isn't the school responsible for too much already? Why should we have to teach the social skills too?"

"These are just little children. Isn't this premature?"

Such are the legitimate questions that arise whenever the topic of building a caring, cooperative classroom erupts in the faculty lounge. Each deserves a thoughtful response.

Why build a caring, cooperative classroom? Why teach students how to cooperate? There are several valid answers. Each answer may not fit every school. But all describe contributing reasons. In our day and age, each reason merits consideration.

1. **The dissolution of the "traditional" family**. Sociologists have documented the increasing numbers of children who come from single-parent, mixed-parent, dual working-parent, and no-parent homes. We can now add the homeless child as well. They tell us that in today's world, these family structures are the norm, not the rare exception. These same sociologists have shown us the effects that the different family structures may have on student achievement and behavior in school. Most experienced teachers can corroborate those effects. And most parents, especially those who must raise children as the sole parent or as dual working parents, know the special challenges and unique child-rearing problems they experience. Probably nothing is more difficult than the lack of time these parents have for their youngsters. The time to support, assist, correct, model positive values, communicate expected behavior, and encourage social skills is often not there, not because the parents are bad, but because they are struggling to earn the dollars to keep the family fed and clothed. Add the decreased time and energy for proper supervision and the result is more students arriving at the schoolhouse door without the basic social skills in place.

2. **TV models**. The change in family structure can account for only a small portion of the rationale for teaching social skills in the schoolhouse. However, when we combine the enormous number of hours that young people sit in front of the TV each week with the decrease of adult supervision, support, and direction, we can see readily why the electronic babysitter has such a negative influence on young minds. The TV, with its aptitude for modeling the most anti-social, anti-caring behaviors, has filled a void in the character formation of today's youth.

If the child wants to learn how adults learn to laugh, he or she needs only to copy the art of the put-down in today's situation comedies and cartoon shows. If the child wants to learn how adults solve problems, he or she needs only to watch the horror movies and the detective shows to master the arts of "shoot-em-down" or "beat-em-up." Love and kindness? Cooperation? Just review the soaps. Mutual support or caring? Try "family" shows such as the Simpsons. Given the average student's average ingestion of TV it is a wonder that any positive behavior occurs on the playground or in the classroom.

3. **Unclear value focus in the school**. In pursuit of our nation's desire to provide equal educational opportunity for all who come to the schoolhouse door, the desire to be free of religious influence inside the schoolhouse has caused our public schools to adopt a value-empty philosophy. This in turn has left most public schools without any focus on what is most important for students to learn. As so

many studies on school excellence have argued, a school without a focus is like a ship without a rudder. In place of the positive value focus, an "every man for himself" philosophy is dominant. In such an environment, young people become confused and unclear. In this state, they learn little about social responsibility, mutual caring, respect, or cooperation.

These three factors have contributed greatly to the increased number of students who have little idea about how to behave in a social organization, other than what they have learned from the negative social models that saturate their lives. As the number of these students increases, the amount of attention that a teacher can give to the academic work in school diminishes. More time is spent on correcting negative behavior, stopping for interruptions, and managing conflicts.

If the American school is going to adhere to the ideal that every child be educated to the fullest of his or her potential, the problems and challenges created by the changing world in which both students and schools exist must be addressed. The school, and more specifically, the classroom teacher, can only do so much. Given this unique challenge and given the limited resources and the increasing pressures on education, the teacher and the school must start with what they can most control: instructional time and proven methods that address the problems which most regularly block quality instruction time.

The methods for teaching cooperative social skills have not only proven their worth (Johnson and Johnson, 1989; Cohen et al., 1990), but also provided a framework for intensifying academic achievement, fostering higher-order thinking, and extending learning into new dimensions for all learners (Joyce, Showers, and Rolheiser-Bennett, 1987).

What all this says to us is that in spite of the changes in children that teachers see each day, the tools do exist to counteract the problems and to move students to the high levels of learning that teachers have always desired. The task of moving students to higher levels of learning will require that we re-order instructional priorities, restructure curriculum, and reschedule time.

The answer to "why social skills," therefore, does not mean that a teacher has to cover less of his or her academic curriculum: it does mean that he or she will spend more time getting students ready for their academic work by taking some extra time in the beginning of the school year to change behaviors and attitudes. When the teacher takes the time at the start of the year to work on cooperative social skills, the students dig into the academic work more deeply with fewer interruptions and more time on task. Like the "little engine that could," the teacher puts a great deal more energy into getting the train to roll, but much less energy once the train is roaring down the tracks.

Those are the short-range and practical reasons for taking time to focus on cooperative social skills. The other, more long-range reasons have to do with the paradigm shift our society is experiencing with more intensity each year. That shift has the world moving from a highly individualistic "me-first" social structure to a "we-sink-or-swim-together" structure.

We see the shift all around us. For instance, we see how most major corporations weave teamwork, quality circles, vertical decision teams, and other "we" approaches to participatory management into the fabric of their organizations. In several of the top MBA programs, students are assigned team projects, work for team grades, and are evaluated for their team contributions. The international economy requires business transactions with people of very diverse cultures. Success in the shrinking global economy depends very much on finely tuned people skills.

How can a teacher build a caring, cooperative classroom?

Creating a caring, cooperative classroom is a major teaching challenge. First, the attitudes promoted in the cooperative classroom run counter to the put-down, competitive culture of most schools and most communities. Second, attitudes and beliefs don't change easily. Many students are deeply mired in negative, non-cooperative behaviors learned from TV, the street, and their peer culture. Third, the effort and time needed to produce the change is hard to find in the already full teaching day. But, it can be done! As Alfie Kohn (1991), Jeannie Oakes and Martin Lipton (1991), and other authors point out there are a host of exemplary classroom models in which caring and cooperation are the rule. James Comer's work, IRI's Project Extend, and classrooms in West Virginia, Oklahoma, and California show that it is possible for even the most difficult and at-risk students to learn cooperative behaviors and develop caring attitudes.

In this book, we use the "best practices" developed in Project Extend by a team of cooperative learning consultants and in the classrooms of Lawton, Oklahoma. Project Extend, funded by the U.S. Department of Education's "Follow Through" Program, worked three years in five school districts in northern Illinois. In that time, teachers and principals learned how to use cooperative learning as the critical instructional tool. Special emphasis was placed on teaching the K-3 students how to work cooperatively, how to care about classmates, and how to respect themselves, their teachers, and their parents. Parents also learned to work with the cooperative framework and to reinforce the "we take care of each other" attitudes.

This book presents a curriculum of social skills, a teaching methodology, and specific lessons drawn from the experience of the classroom teachers. When we have taught these strategies to other teachers, they have reported similar results to our Follow Through project: (1) emphasis on the social skill model that asks students, even very young ones, to practice, self evaluate, and refine, changed teaching methods from passive to active learning; (2) active learning in the lessons helped students find new ways to interact with each other, build team spirit and caring for each other; and (3) parents reported positive changes in their children's behavior and attitudes at home.

When is it best to start social skill development?

A well-conceived early childhood program ought to be saturated with social skill instruction and opportunity for the young students to practice as they play together. Unfortunately, all such programs are not so well conceived. In some programs, more and more academic content is forced at earlier and earlier ages to such a degree that this rich opportunity for social skill formation is eliminated. In others, the students play randomly, sometimes alone and sometimes together. The ideal program, even at the pre-school stage, would provide some modeling, guided practice, and constructive feedback in cooperative social skills, along with language development and fun activities that make learning an active engagement for all students.

This social skill instruction cannot end with graduation into the primary grades. If anything, the primary grades can be the best opportunity for young students to develop fully the foundation of social skills which will ensure academic success and positive self-esteem in the later years. And, as the students move into the middle grades where peer pressure is so strong, the encouragement and support *must* continue.

Some upper grade people will argue that today's students didn't have this foundation. Thus, they say, it is a waste of time to start now. Nothing could be further from the truth. Although it may be more difficult to introduce students already formed with negative social skills to the values of cooperation, trust, and respect, it is never too late. In fact, it is probably all the more important to take the extra time and introduce the social skills even in the 12th grade if that is what the students most need.

What is the best way to teach social skills?

Social skill instruction works best in a direct instruction transfer model. This model, as we have used it here in this book, calls for six key ingredients in its recipe for success.

1. **The hook or set**. This is a "hands-on" classroom experience that engages the students in what the cooperative social skill looks like and sounds like. The activity works best when it is content-free, fun, and engages all the students. For primary students we have utilized a large number of award-winning videos that will stimulate student interest and lead to fruitful understanding. In addition, there are hands-on activities which serve as lab experiences for the children to observe and assess their own use of the social skills they are learning. These in-class experiences provide a foundation that fills in the "prior knowledge" void with which these students enter the classroom. Once the void is filled, they can build their learning on a solid foundation.

2. **The lesson**. After each "hook" activity, the children will reflect on what they did and said in the activity. Aided by the teacher's questions, the children will develop one or two lists. List one will identify specific behaviors (words and actions) of the non-example (e.g., put-downs are the non-examples of giving encouragement). They may construct a second list of the exemplary behaviors (i.e., what words and actions encourage a person). Both lists are posted and labeled as acceptable or not acceptable. Whenever possible, companion lists that identify how someone might feel when treated with the OK and not OK behaviors can be posted.

ENCOURAGEMENT	
SOUNDS LIKE	LOOKS LIKE
"Keep at it."	thumbs up
"Atta girl," "Atta boy!"	pat on back
"Way to go!"	smile
"Here's another way to look at it…"	head nodding
"Great idea."	beckoning hand
"Keep trying."	
"You're getting close."	

3. **Practice or follow-up**. Massed practice (short, intense, and frequent) of the targeted behaviors follow the list-making lesson. At least once a day for five to seven minutes, structured and explicit practice of the behaviors will cement the social skill and make it a normal behavior. Social skill practices work well as a daily

sponge activity at the beginning of the elementary day. They also work as a sponge to close a day. As you will see in the sample lessons, the best massed practices are content-free, focused on the acceptable behaviors, and receive positive reinforcement for their display. Throughout the massed practices, it is best to keep the behavior charts for the social skill displayed on poster board or as a bulletin board. With these cues visible all the time, the students who might forget or elect to ignore the behaviors during the day can be easily reminded of what is and what is not acceptable behavior.

When it becomes evident that the students are becoming comfortable with the social skill in the artificial practice (this usually takes several weeks with some re-teaching and an occasional new "hook"), it is time to imbed the skill practice into daily content lessons.

4. **Reflection, discussion, or closure**. As soon as the practices begin, it is best for students to also start their "look backs" and reflections on their practice of the social skills. At least once a week during the massed practice, it is best for students to spend time in structured reflections. At this time, they are asked to look back at their use of the targeted skills and discuss what they have learned about the social skill or its use, how much improvement they are making with the social skill, and how they might improve more. When the social skill is imbedded in the lesson, it is helpful for them to reflect on how the use of the social skill is helping the small group, how the skill practice can be improved, other places to use the same skill, and how group members can help each other further develop the skill.

5. **Feedback, recognition, and celebration**. As the students demon-strate improvement in the use of the targeted social skill, private and public feedback on progress is a powerful tool. The four steps identified above create perfect opportunities for "catching students doing good things."

Some teachers keep a classroom chart, marking all instances of appropriate use of the targeted social skill by each student; others chart the progress of the class as a whole. Some teachers use bean jars on each group's table to track each group's progress. Others hand out certificates when individuals or groups demonstrate marked improvement. Easiest of all, of course, is when the teacher stops by a group and affirms the positive behavior in very specific terms: "I like how this group is keeping its voices low by having only one person speak at a time." Note that the reinforcing feedback focuses on the group's use of the skill under practice.

Skill / Student	Calling each other by name	Giving compli- ments	Staying with group	Following instructions
Sue	x	x	x	
Tom	x	x	xxx	x
Kyle	x		x	x
Mary	x	xx	x	x

To go along with the positive feedback, all-class recognition of social skill improvement and classroom celebrations for multiple successes are even more helpful for promoting transfer inside and outside the classroom. (Contrast the positive effect of writing a student's name or a group's name on the blackboard for demonstrating attentive use of a cooperative social skill to the writing of a student's name for disruptive behavior.) From simple "hurrahs" to certificates, popcorn parties and earned time for every group that demonstrates growth in the day-to-day use of the targeted social skill, there are many options to let groups know that they deserve recognition for a job well done.

6. **Transfer**. To help students transfer the targeted social skill outside the classroom to the cafeteria, gym, playground, bus, and home, it helps if there is an all-school plan for recognizing classes that excel in using the skills throughout the school. It matters little whether classroom points are tabulated with precision or the staff votes on successful applications (this is not a competition; all classes that meet the application criteria outside the classroom walls deserve recognition). What matters is that the cooperative behavior is noticed, that recognition is made public to the rest of the students, faculty, and parents, and that students continue to reflect on their own positive behavior.

Within the classroom, transfer is much easier. By selecting one or two units per school year, the teacher can have ample time to reinforce and extend the use of each social skill into every lesson in the classroom. The behavior charts mentioned above are an easy means to encourage children to practice the social skills all day long. Thus, once the children show understanding of a social skill, the attendant behaviors, the skill's value inside and outside the classroom, and once they begin to use it automatically, it is imperative that the teacher imbed the skill in every cooperative lesson. This is possible with little difficulty and no loss of time. At the beginning of each lesson, no matter what the content, the teacher will cue the class to attend to the practiced skill. By adding an incentive such as bonus points, a group reward, or the opportunity for the groups to assess the use of the skill, the teacher will heighten the students' attention to practice of that skill.

Which social skills should be stressed?

The possibilities are endless. However, there are several cooperative social skills that may be more helpful to students and teachers alike in starting the school experience. As we have outlined in Unit One in this book, these foundation skills are (1) calling each other by name (2) forming small groups (3) attending to instructions (4) giving compliments. From a practical perspective, these are the skills that ensure basic management in the cooperative classroom. With these in place, the students can advance to learning the basic behaviors and attitudes of cooperation, teamwork, social responsibility, friendship, conflict resolution, and problem solving.

Given the shortage of time, is there a way to integrate social skills into content? The answer is "yes and no." The most proven way to teach social skills is to start with an explicit lesson on the skill. As described above, this will include a "hook" activity so that the students have an immediate experience from which to work and on which they can model their own behavior. It will also include the development of behavior lists, guided practice, reinforcement of the acceptable behaviors, and reflection/self-assessment time. As we have designed these lessons for this book, this sequence should take no more than thirty minutes from the average classroom plus as much follow-up time as the class may need to make the skills second nature. It is far better to spend a year cementing one social skill than to "cover" twenty to get ready for a test. These are skills for a lifetime, not for a test. Thus, the "no" part of the answer is that before a teacher can integrate the social skills into the curriculum, it is best to teach an explicit social skill lesson free of any content and then expect its regular use day in and day out.

But don't forget the "yes" part of the answer. A teacher using sound instructional practices can shorten the time needed for integrating the social skills into the curriculum. In the primary grades, that speed-up may be easier and quicker than in the upper grades, especially if the idea is to practice and perfect a few skills rather than "cover" ten or twenty during the year.

We have integrated most of the material on social skills into lessons that are designed to develop reading, thinking, listening, and speaking skills through a variety of media.

1.   The social skills provide a thematic bond for the reading of *literature*. Using video and print versions of classic myths, folk tales, and fables as models, children are exposed to literature as the springboard for learning about social skills. The children are invited to examine the characters in the story and draw life lessons from the ways these literary characters solve problems and interact with others. (See page 117 for the list of videos.)

2.   Throughout the lessons, index cards are used to label objects and to construct lists of words for *choral reading*. Overheads with simple instructions, bulletin boards with single-word procedures, and other easy-to-read methods are provided to extend oral reading opportunities throughout each lesson. In the choral reading, the teacher sounds out names attached to persons or objects and then leads the class as a chorus to practice saying the words.

3.   The stronger readers in the class are grouped with children with lesser developed skills. The *readers are encouraged to read* as others in the small group follow along in a single text. In like manner, many of the lessons are structured for the teacher to read aloud to the class. This does not mean that the weaker readers never read. As the students bond in their groups, it is advisable to rotate the reader and foster encouragement of fellow group members.

4.   Many activities invite the student groups to *complete stories* or make parallel stories to enact in puppet shows or live drama for the class, other classes, or parents.

5.   Group activities are structured so that every student has the opportunity to *summarize ideas, stories, or decisions* and explain why the group decided as it did. By building in instructional strategies such as wait time, equal distribution of responses, the wraparound, fat questions, and all-student cueing, the likelihood that all students will become involved is increased.

6.   *Graphic organizers* are used as the tools to initiate thinking about the stories the children read in the lessons. Special attention is devoted to attribute webs which enable students who are visual learners to organize their thinking about the stories.

7. Each lesson calls for a variety of *higher-order questions* for individual and group responses. These are there to promote student thinking about the content and how the content of the stories may transfer to the classroom or to other places in the children's lives.

8. *Drama, art, and games* are used to create hands-on learning experiences that promote the transfer of learning from the stories to the children's life experiences outside the classroom.

9. For each key lesson provided, there are suggestions for *follow-up activity*. The suggestions reinforce the skills and can be used in many types of lessons. The more encouragement and follow-up, the more deeply will the social skill become imbedded in school culture.

How often and when?

This book is designed to enable use of the lessons in several different ways. One way to use this book is to select one unit per semester per grade level. Do one lesson a month. Before you imbed the skill by using at least one cooperative lesson a day in another content area (e.g., math, science, PE), use the follow-up lessons as the "bridge" for students to key into what you expect from them. Encourage the children to practice the social skill as much as possible with the bulletin board, incentives, and evaluation of their improved use of the selected social skill. Although it will be helpful to use Unit One to start each new year in the lowest grades, there are enough units to use the lessons in this sequence:

Kindergarten: Units one and two
Grade One: Units one and three
Grade Two: Units one and four
Grade Three: Units one, five and six

Another way to use this book, after spending the first half of Kindergarten on Unit One, is to work on one lesson a month from each of the other units. Each year after, repeat what is needed from Unit One to start a new class and take a different lesson from each unit.

When do we see the results?

At first, even the young students resist this shift in expectations. They feel uncomfortable. The older students will feel "phoney" before their peers. However, as you reinforce expected cooperative behaviors, you will see the changing norms. Once you have the "critical mass," more students than not treating each other with care and respect, you will know you have a strong foundation. Each year continue adding your bricks, mortar, beams, frame, and roof.

What is the best way to assess student development in social skills?

For the primary grades, use of the behavior T charts will make it easy for you to track individual progress. By outlining the specific behaviors you want the students to develop, you also create the format for behavior check lists.

LISTENING	
LOOKS LIKE	SOUNDS LIKE

When it comes time to report this progress to parents either on a formal report card or in an informal summary, you can communicate progress on the basis of increased incidents of the desired behaviors or in comparison to standards. To set the standards, decide how many instances of desired behaviors you would label as "outstanding," how many for "steady," and how few for "not yet." If you must give a grade, write the name of the social skill that is the semester focus or use a more generic "cooperation" label. Assign a letter or number grade appropriate to the number of incidents.

	LETTER	NUMBER	SYMBOL
Listening	A	92	+
Encouraging	B	84	X
Doing Tasks	A	93	+
Caring	C	79	—

In addition to the behavior measure, it is helpful to make a portfolio of student work. This may include a "Cooperation Journal" with a weekly entry that focuses on what the child believes he or she has done well in using the social skills, copies of artifacts from the child's group work, and observation notes about the child's use of social skills in the classroom.

GETTING STARTED

To start a cooperative classroom, it is best to begin with those social skills that will initiate the children to effective group work. These are the skills that they will need to start to work together and initiate the idea of "all for one and one for all." Although the first skills we introduce here may seem simplistic, for young children who are leaving the self-centered period of early childhood and moving into the first other-centered world of the classroom, for children not used to working in a give-and-get environment, these first lessons will be a significant challenge. How much time and practice you devote to the development of these basic social skills will depend on the children themselves. Some will arrive in your classroom with the attitudes and self-concepts needed to adapt easily to the expectations of working in a unit; others will need a great deal of nurture and care before you can wean them from a self-centered, "me first, last, and always" life view to the more "other-centered" way of behaving endemic to the cooperative classroom.

We have observed that in classrooms with children of the very poor and with children of the very rich, classrooms in the large cities and classrooms in the farmlands, classrooms with experienced teachers and classrooms with the novices, time spent to ensure that these basic social skills are in place is time as importantly spent as with the basic reading and math skills. These basic social skills ready the child for success in all social environments, from the classroom to the board room. These are the skills that prepare the child to work with other children, no matter how different or difficult those others may be. These are the skills that lay the foundation for surviving and succeeding in the rough give-and-take of the world outside the school walls. Most importantly, these are the skills that the child will most need in learning how to deal with the complex social challenges and conflicts that will emerge in future school years.

Lesson 1

What's In a Name?

Materials

index cards, colored dots, newsprint, crayons, masking tape

Set

Introduce yourself by printing your name on the board (e.g., Mr. John Smith). Sound out your name and have the class do a choral reading with your direction. Invite them to call you by your title and last name.

Objective

Explain to the class how important it is to call people by their names, and that in this lesson they will learn each other's names.

Lesson

1. Give each child one third of a "people card." Each third of a people card has on it a colored dot (red, green, or yellow) and a letter. Tell the children to find two other parts of the people card (same letter, different color). They will form groups of three. (Show a model group of three and count off each child in the group: "One, two, three.") In the group of three, all must have the same letter and

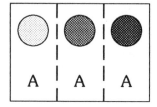

three different colored dots. (Show red, yellow, and green.) Signal the class to start. As groups of three are formed, instruct those groups to sit down together. Help those who are having difficulty until all groups are seated where you want them.

2. Invite the children with the red piece to come to the materials table and pick up a sheet of newsprint and some crayons.

3. Each child is to sketch a self-portrait on the sheet. Be sure that the groups decide on how much space for each member. They must also decide if they are all going to sketch at once or take turns. They may help each other, but they may not say any "bad talk" about each other's sketch. (Some examples of bad talk are: "That looks dumb," "That's stupid," or "Mine is nicer than yours.")

4. As they are drawing, give each child an index card with the child's first name printed on it and a piece of tape. If some children cannot print their own names, someone else may or they may affix the index cards to their sketch.

5. Invite each group to stand up. As the students with the red and yellow dots hold the newsprint, the student with the green dot will introduce all three group members. Encourage the class to give each group applause or a hurrah after its introduction. Post the completed sketches.

Discussion

Ask the class how it felt working together on the task. Encourage a variety of students to respond. If they start to repeat each other's responses, ask for the next ones to think of a different word to describe how they were feeling.

Closure

Give each child an index name card to wear for the rest of the day. Sit the children in a circle. Invite the children to share their name as they show their card. After a child has shared his or her name, lead the class in a choral answer to the following: "What is his or her name?" "Her or his name is_____." Emphasize that you want them to call each other by the given name.

Follow-up

Repeat the name circle each day until the children form the habit of calling each other by their first names. For variety, have teams introduce each other. Ask only the question "What is his or her name?" without modeling the response. You may want to see how many people each student can name. For this, have a volunteer walk behind the circle and name each child in turn. When the child misses a name, he or she sits down and another volunteer takes over.

Lesson 2

Happy Talk

Materials

empty wastebasket, "Hurtful Words" sign and tape, index cards, crayons, blank newsprint, tape

Set

Set a wastebasket on top of your desk. Label it "Hurtful Words." Read the label to the class. Ask volunteers to give you samples of words that people use that hurt their feelings. As a child gives a word, write the word on an index card, show it to the class and then deposit it with flair into the wastebasket.

Objective

Explain to the children that this lesson will focus on putting all words that hurt into the wastebasket so that only "happy talk" is heard in this classroom.

Lesson

1. On a large sheet of newsprint, show the international "not allowed" sign 🚫 . Explain to the children what the sign means. Tell them

that in this classroom they cannot use the hurtful words that you threw away. Take the cards from the wastebasket, and tape them on the sign. Ask if there any more words to put on the sign. Fill it up and post it for all to see.

2. Post a second sheet with a giant yellow sun and many rays. Ask the children what words they hear that make them feel happy. Write the examples on index cards and tape each one to a ray of the sun. It's OK to put several on one ray. Read each word to the class and then guide a choral response.

3. Ask the class why they think these happy words fit on the sun (they make you feel warm, they make you feel happy, etc.). Explain that you want the children to use these happy words when they talk to each other in class.

Discussion

Ask the children to explain why they think it is better to use happy talk than to use hurtful words. Ask for as many different ideas as they can generate in three to five minutes.

Closure

Ask the children to turn to a neighbor, shake hands, and say one nice thing about that person. After this is done, give the class some happy talk and encourage them to keep giving happy messages to each other throughout the day, week, and school year.

Follow-up

Each time a child uses a hurtful word, write the word on an index card and have the child drop it into the wastebasket. Develop an easy reward system for using happy talk. For example, stickers, pats on the back, giving class hurrahs. Have a moment of happy talk once or twice a day. Stop the class activity and tell the children to turn to a neighbor and use happy talk.

Lesson
3

handwritten notes:
jig saw
- use purnples
- have groups put
together
- process - 1 person
from each group.

One, Two, Three

Materials

index cards

Set

Ask the children how many have ever worked together in a small group in the classroom. Count the raised hands. Ask some of those who raised a hand to tell what they did in the small group. Explain to the children that in this class they will work many times in small groups. They will do that so that they can learn how to work with other students, whether they are friends or not.

Objective

In this lesson, the students are going to learn the three steps for rearranging the desks for small-group work.

Lesson

1. Tell the children that at the count of one, all students are to stand up next to their desks without talking.
2. Count "One."

3. As soon as all are standing without talking, tell the children that at the count of two, each should group with two other students and turn their desks into a group of three. Before giving the signal, walk among the desks and place a letter card on each desk. Have three Xs, three Ys, etc. (or however many groups of three you'll have). Place the cards so that the children have an easy move. Show them how to pick up the desk and turn it into the group of three.

4. Count "Two." As the children are moving the desks, encourage them to work quietly. After each pair moves the first desk, they need to look around and see who may need assistance. When all desks are in place and no one needs help, the children should stand by their desks without talking.

5. As soon as all have returned to stand by their desks without talking, tell them to sit at their desks at the three count.

Discussion

Ask the children if there are any questions about the moving task. Compliment the class on the steps they did well. Point out the steps that they will need to practice and improve. (You can repeat the practice as much as you feel necessary.) When you feel that they can do the sequence by a simple announcement that you are going to use the three count for moving desks, reduce the commands to one, two, three. Remind the students of what you will expect to see. Keep a list if necessary (e.g., no talking, help others).

Closure

Ask for a volunteer to repeat the instructions for moving into small groups. Ask other volunteers to help if the child gets stuck or forgets something.

Follow-up

When the quality of performance of this three-step procedure drops, go back to the step-by-step instructions. When the procedure becomes second nature, invite different students to give the count and monitor the tasks.

Lesson

4

Nonverbal Communication book

Stop, Look, and Listen

Materials

overhead (p. 88)

Set

Show the "Stop, Look, and Listen" overhead (p.88). Invite the children to tell you what the signs mean. When you get the correct answer for each, write the word under the sign and lead the class in a choral reading of each word.

Objective

Explain to the children that in this lesson they are going to learn one signal for stopping, looking, and listening in this classroom.

Lesson

1. Hold up your right hand. Instruct all the children do the same.
2. Have everyone drop their hands. Tell the children that they are going to learn a very old signal used by the Girl Scouts since 1910. When a student sees the teacher's hand raised or lots of students'

hands, the student is to *stop* talking or doing the task and raise his or her own hand, *look* at the teacher, and *listen* for the next instruction.

3. Check for understanding by asking several different children to explain how to stop, look, and listen, each in the student's own words.

4. Practice the procedure and give constructive feedback.

Discussion

Ask the children to explain the reasons why they think the procedure to stop, look, and listen is important in the classroom.

Closure

Thank the children for their cooperation and invite them to stop, look, and listen each time they see your hand go up as a signal.

Follow-up

When some of the children forget to follow the procedure or keep talking as they raise their hands, go back and check for understanding and give guided practice. Be extra careful not to give instructions or discuss a point with the class until all the children are looking and listening to you.

Watch Your Manners, Please

Materials

overhead (p. 89), bulletin board

Set

Ask the children if any know the meaning of the word *rude*. Invite those who know to give an example of someone who is rude on television. What does that person do or say? (If there are no volunteers, select a current example from television.) Discuss how a student would show rudeness in class or the lunchroom (for example, talking out of turn, line-butting, saying mean words).

Objective

Explain to the children that in today's lesson they are going to learn some ways to show good manners and not be rude in a group.

Lesson

1. On the overhead (p. 89), show the following list of good manners for a work group.

> **GOOD GROUP MANNERS**
> - Stay with the group.
> - One person talks at a time.
> - Use six-inch voices.*
> - Do your job.
> - Use first names.
> - Be a cheerleader.

2. Read each item or invite a strong reader to read each item. Have the children do a choral response.

3. Ask for volunteers to explain what they think each item means. Solicit a variety of students to comment. When a child gives an acceptable response, reinforce the response and then go on to the next item.

Discussion

Invite the children to tell why they think each of the items is important for good manners. Solicit several responses to each by asking, "And why else does that show good manners?"

Closure

Thank the children for their good ideas in the discussion. Unveil the bulletin board with the six good manners in a list. Tell the children that these are the behaviors that you will look for whenever the class works in small groups.

Follow-up

Before each group activity, review the list either by leading the class in a choral reading or by asking different children to read items from the list. On certain days you may want to highlight one of the items by giving bonus points to the groups who show special ability to follow that guideline.

---

*low voices, audible only to one who is no more than six inches away from the speaker

FRIENDSHIP

What makes a true friend? This is a question every child asks in each stage of development. It is not an easy question to answer. However, it is important. The answer requires not only discovering what the attributes of a friend are, but also how to put the attributes into practice. Each of the lessons that follows is designed to help children identify the qualities of a friend before putting into practice those qualities in their own lives.

Lesson 1

Making Friends

Materials

crayons, newsprint, "The Lion and the Mouse" video (see p. 117), TV, video recorder, or story

Set

Have the children sit in pairs. Give each pair some crayons and a sheet of newsprint. Invite each pair to draw a picture of two friends doing something together. After they have drawn their pictures, invite the pairs to show their pictures and to share some ideas of what they think makes a real friend. Affirm the responses and print the key words on the board or on a large sheet of newsprint for all to see. After you have a list of seven to ten words, go back over the list with a choral response. Model each word and then have the class repeat your pronunciation. Tell the class that the words they just pronounced are words that some people use to describe a good friend.

Objective

Tell the children that today's lesson is to learn about how to be a friend.

Lesson

1. Tell the children that they are going to study a story about two animals who became friends: the lion and the mouse. After the story, they will have the chance to tell how the two animals were friends.

2. Show the video "The Lion and the Mouse" or read the story to the class.

3. After the story is over, draw a double T-Chart on the board or on newsprint.

FRIENDSHIP

LOOKS LIKE	SOUNDS LIKE	FEELS LIKE

4. Discuss what the three column headings mean.

5. Ask the children to give you examples of things the lion or mouse *did* to show friendship. Enter these in the "Looks Like" column. Repeat for things the animals *said* that showed friendship. Enter these in the "Sounds Like" column. Make sure that all in the class agree an item belongs on the chart.

6. Ask for ideas on what the children think friendship felt like to the lion and the mouse. Enter these in the "Feels Like" column. Encourage the children to explain why they chose their answers.

7. When the children run out of ideas, you may add some examples of your own.

8. Put up a second double T-Chart. Label it "Not Friends" or "Enemies." Repeat the process with examples from the story.

NOT FRIENDS

LOOKS LIKE	SOUNDS LIKE	FEELS LIKE

Discussion

Have the children face their partners with their drawings. Invite the pairs to talk about how their pictures of friendship are like the friendship of the lion and the mouse, or how they are different. Invite several pairs to show their drawings and share their ideas. Give strong affirmations.

Closure

Have the children sign their first names to their pair drawings. Post the drawings.

Follow-up

Select some additional stories from the library in which friendship is the theme. Read these to the children and encourage them to add words to the double T-Charts.

Lesson 2

Friendship Story

Materials

lion and mouse puppets (see p. 100), popsicle sticks, crayons, glue, tape, cloth scraps, newsprint, Friendship double T-Chart

Set

Copy the lion and mouse puppets onto cardboard. Cut them out, decorate them, and attach them to a popsicle stick. Invent your dialogue for the following scenario:

Lion: Thank the mouse for helping him escape.

Mouse: Explain how it is important for friends to help each other.

Lion: Use double T-Chart from Lesson 1 to review the characteristics of a friend.

Mouse: Review the good feelings that go with friendship.

Lion: Explain how he would help the mouse if a cat trapped her family.

Mouse: Ask the children why they thought the lion's answer showed he was a friend.

Objective

After the children have shared their answers to the mouse's question, explain that in today's lesson they are going to make their own puppets and a play that shows the mouse and the lion's friendship.

Lesson

1. Divide the children into pairs. Designate the shorter child in each pair to be the lion, the taller to be the mouse. Give each pair cut-out puppets (duplicate masters on p. 100) and scraps of material.

2. Invite them to agree on the colors for each puppet and to color the puppets.

3. After the pairs are finished, have each pair work together on each puppet, gluing each and attaching the material. (Demonstrate the steps for all to see and then coach the pairs.) Have each pair sign both puppets.

4. When all are ready, have the pairs show their puppets to the class. (This is a good spot for a break. Store the puppets for use the next day.)

5. (Redistribute the puppet sets.) Explain to the class that you are going to give them a story to complete. It will be a new story to show the friendship of the lion and the mouse. Each pair will make up its own ending to the story and all will have a chance to share the endings.

6. Start the story: "One day while the mouse was walking her children in the forest, she found a big hole. It was very long and very deep (show 12 inches long and 6 inches deep), or at least so it seemed to the tiny mice. Mrs. Mouse told her children to stay away from the edge. The youngest mouse didn't listen and fell right in. While the mother mouse was trying to figure out how to get the baby out, she heard a loud thump, and then another thump. She looked up and saw a giant hunter coming toward her. Quickly, she helped the other little mice to hide in the tall grass. Before she could return to the baby, the hunter bent over the hole and picked the baby out. Mrs. Mouse didn't know what to do. She took the rest of her family and scurried off to find her friend, the lion. The lion had just finished dinner. Mrs. Mouse told her story. The lion listened. Finally, he said, 'I know just what to do. Because you are my friend, I will help you.'"

7. Stop the story here. Instruct the pairs to take up the story and to include the following: first, the lion will tell the mouse what his plan is. Next, he will go off while Mrs. Mouse tells why the lion is a good friend. Then he will come back with the rescued baby and tell what he did. Mrs. Mouse will thank him. Put the following sequence on the board so the pairs can refer to it as they practice.

| Lion tells the plan. | Mouse explains their friendship. | Lion tells the rescue. | Mouse says thank you. |

8. Give each lion a cut-out baby mouse to bring back (duplicate master on p. 100).

9. After the pairs practice, select volunteers to act out their puppet story. After each story, ask other students to tell what they liked about the story or how the lion showed his friendship. (This is a good spot for a break.)

10. Over the next few days, invite other students to share their stories and to receive feedback from the class.

Discussion

After all who wish to have done their puppet stories, invite the children to share some situations in which their friends have shown friendship. Students may also wish to share ways in which they themselves showed friendship to others.

Closure

On the board, create a list of ways the students helped each other as they made the puppets and the plays. Prime the pump by giving some examples you noticed as you watched the pairs work. Ask volunteers to add to the list.

Follow-up

Help the children make new puppets that represent themselves. Each pair will select one real-life situation showing how someone was a friend to them. Allow time for practice then have the pairs present the plays to the class.

Lesson 3

A Secret Friend

Materials

Friendship Award Certificates (p. 101), name cards, Friendship double T-Chart

Set

Review the Friendship double T-Chart from Lesson 1 with the class.

Objective

Tell the children that they are going to work on being good friends by practicing all the ways to be a friend that are on the chart and by watching how others are good friends.

Lesson

1. Show the Friendship Award Certificate (see p. 101 for a master).

Tell the students that each day this week they each will have a different secret friend to watch. At the end of each day, they will give their secret friend a special Friendship Award.

2. Explain how they will watch for a friendly act or listen for friendly words by their secret friend. (Show examples on a double T-chart.) At the end of the day, they will fill in the name of their secret friend and words to describe what that friend did or said from the double T-chart. Distribute a secret friend name to each child. (You will repeat this procedure each day with a different name given to each child each day.)

3. At the end of the day, give each child a blank certificate. Have the children fill in the blanks with the friend's name they received that morning and the friendship behavior from the double T-chart. Have the students exchange the certificates after they sign their own names.

Discussion

Invite the children to share with the class why it is important to be a friend.

Closure

At the end of the week, put the children into groups of three. Let the children read their awards to the trio. After all are read, the trio should look to see how many of their awards are alike. After all trios find their similar awards, allow each trio to select one similarity to share with the class. Give each trio a hurrah after it has shared.

Follow-up

Have the children go on a daily friendship hunt. Tell them to watch for ways others show friendship that day. At the end of the day, seat the students in a circle and ask volunteers to describe what they saw (without names).

Lesson 4

Friendship Mobile

Materials

scissors, tub of paste, magazines, metal clothes hangers, geometric cards (cut out circles, triangles, squares, etc. from cardboard or index cards), twine, Friendship double T-Chart, newsprint, marker, friend outline overhead (p. 90)

Set

Put the children into new groups of three. The child wearing the most blue in each group will get the scissors, one tub of paste, three magazines, a metal clothes hanger, six pre-cut geometric cards, and two feet of pre-cut twine from the materials table. While this child is getting the materials, the other two will review the Friendship double T-Chart and tell how they have been a good friend this week.

Objective

When the groups are settled with the materials, tell them that they are going to make a friendship mobile.

Lesson

1. Show the children a completed mobile. Explain how you put it together. Pass it around for the groups to examine.

2. The child who picked up the materials (the child wearing the most blue) will lay out the magazines. The child to the right of this student will help look for pictures that show friendship. The third child will cut out the pictures picked by the others. (Allow 10 minutes.)

3. Each group will work together to paste the pictures on the geometric cards. Using the twine, they will balance the cards from the hanger as well as possible. Coach as needed.

4. After the pictures are attached, each group must agree on how it will explain how it selected its picture, and then sign the completed mobile.

5. Hang the mobiles. Each day, select several groups to explain their friendship pictures.

Discussion

After all groups have had the chance to explain their friendship pictures, use the mobiles to make a class list of all the places and times being a good friend is important. Put their ideas on a large sheet of newsprint (this will be their "friend list").

Closure

Display the friend list (above) for all to see. Each group will make a people poem with words that describe a friend. Have the students in each group make a shadow outline of two friends. Invite the groups to use words from the list to fill out the outline.

Have all members in each group sign their group's poem before you post it. After you have hung all the poems, do a class wraparound, encouraging all children to say what they liked best about their work group.

Follow-up

Do other cooperative art projects that focus on friendship (a collage of pictures, water colors, papier-mâché, a classroom mural on newsprint, etc.).

Lesson 5

We Are Best of Friends

Materials

word cards (see below), ad from the newspaper, Friendship double T-Chart, newsprint, crayons or markers

Set

Show the class a full-page ad from the daily paper. Help the children read it. Ask them why they would or would not buy what the ad is selling. Probe their reasons by asking several to explain why or why not.

Objective

Working in pairs and using all that they have been learning about being a friend, the children will make ads about their friends.

Lesson

1. Give each child half of a word that describes friendship. Use the words from the double T-Chart that tells what friendship looks like

and sounds like. (Preprint the words on index cards and then cut the words in half.) Instruct each child to find the matching partner and to sit down in the area you designate.

2. As soon as all are settled, signal for attention. On the board, write the word friendship and sound it out with the class. Ask each pair to agree on how to say its word. Help as needed. Instruct each pair to tape its word(s) on the board. Help the class pronounce the word(s) and then explain the word(s) to the class.

3. On the board or overhead, draw an attribute web (or use the master on p. 91). Show the children how to fill in the web by selecting words from the card list or by adding their own words.

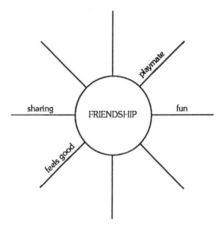

4. Give each pair a sheet of blank paper (preferably 2' x 2') and a marker or crayon. Designate one child to draw the web (child wearing the most blue in each pair). In the middle, the drawer will write the partner's name (he or she will be the focus child). On the web's rays they will take turns writing in the characteristics of the focus child as a friend. Allow eight minutes so they can get as many words written down as they can.

5. At the end of the eight minutes, signal the pairs to stop, look, and listen. Demonstrate on your model web how they are to agree on the three words that most describe this focus person as a friend. They will write those on a sidebar.

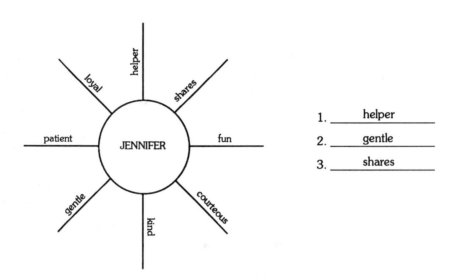

1. _____helper_____

2. _____gentle_____

3. _____shares_____

6. Allow three to five minutes for the pairs to agree on their choices and to write them on the sidebar. After they finish, each pair should sign the sheet. (This is a good spot for a break. Instruct the pairs to roll up or fold the sheets and place them in the spot you designate. Tell them that they will continue tomorrow. Collect the markers and return the children to their seats. Keep the lists and the models available.)

7. (Begin again the next day.) Select four or five pairs to show their webs and to introduce the focus child. The focus child will hold the web for all to see as the other child says, "This is _____. She is a friend because . . ." After each introduction is finished, applaud or give a hurrah. Post the webs. Continue until all are done.

8. After the first half of the class is done, repeat the activity for the second half of each pair. Keep the same pairs.

Discussion

Ask the children to examine the posted webs. Which words appear most often? As you solicit responses, make a new web on the board or overhead to record the words they pick. Ask the class to give you ideas about why they think the words they selected are so important to friendship.

Closure

Do a wraparound and encourage all children in turn to select what they think is their best quality as a friend and why. Model this for them: "I am proud that I am _____ because _____." Encourage all students to listen.

Follow-up

Put the pairs into groups of four. Invite them to make a list of all the friendship qualities shared by all four members in the new group. Encourage each group to share its likenesses. For example, "the new ways we are alike as friends are . . ." As the others wait for a turn to present, invite them to listen for qualities on their list or repeated by other groups. What are the characteristics all children in the class share? Help the class make a list of the characteristics shared by everyone in the class. Make a class bulletin board titled, "The Ways We Are Alike as Friends." Use the words for choral reading practice.

RESPONSIBILITY

Outside the family, the classroom is the first place that a child becomes aware that he or she is not an island, but an integral part of a social group. That group is part of a social order, called the school. The school has rules, privileges, peers, leaders, and subordinates. People live and work together to accomplish set goals and objectives. The more smoothly they work together, the more they all benefit.

The primary grades are the transition grades. The child moves from being "me-centered" to learning how to be "other-centered," without losing his or her individuality. We call this other-centeredness "social responsibility." Social responsibility is knowing what your obligations are in the social unit (the school in this case) and acting to fulfill these obligations. Social responsibility is most advantageous when it springs from within the individual, and not when it is imposed from the outside.

By helping young children develop an understanding of social responsibility and the benefits of the social contract, we lay the foundation for the development of that inner motivation. Children can say, "I am a member of this society and I have responsibilities, as does each other member, to make it work well." Thus, we start in this early unit with lessons that not only develop the concept of responsibility, but also provide concrete experiences to challenge and encourage each child to put those concepts into practice.

Lesson 1

Make A Machine

Materials

index cards, newsprint, markers, tape

Set

Write the word *responsibility* on the board. Sound it out for the class and do a choral reading. Discuss what it means with the class.

Objective

Explain to the children that they are going to learn about the word *responsibility* by working with a group to make a machine.

Lesson

1. Make an open space in the classroom. Mix the students into random groups of seven to nine. Have each group stand in a circle, shoulder to shoulder.

2. Identify the tallest child in each group. That child is number one. Have each group count off to the right of number one. As soon as each has a number, have the highest number from each group get

a set of job cards from you (see below). Adjust the number of cards to fit the number of children in each group. Be sure the song card is assigned in every group.

3. Each child in a group will get one job. If a child cannot read the instructions, encourage other members of the group to help. You should intervene only if no one in the group can read the card.

Make the sound "um-pa-pa" over and over.

Make the sound "ding-dong" over and over.

Make the sound "swish-swish" over and over.

Make the sound "chug-chug" over and over.

Make the sound "rat-a-tat-tat" over and over.

Make the sound "honk-honk" over and over.

Make the sound "clunk-clunk" over and over.

Sing your favorite song.

4. Tell each group that it is to make itself into a machine. All the different parts in the machine will move in a different direction and make a different sound when the machine is on. Let the groups figure out who will move how. The only rule is that they must all move when you say so and stop when you say so. Whenever they are moving, they must make their noises.

5. Allow five minutes for planning and rehearsing the machine. Pick one machine to stop and start as the others watch. Then run the second machine, and so on until all have had a brief run.

6. Tell the children that you are now going to run all the machines at once. Every one must start and stop on your signals. Keep practicing until everyone starts and stops together. Celebrate when this happens.

Discussion

Put a T-chart on the board. Ask the students to tell you what helped and what hindered their machines from working smoothly. List the responses.

Helped (for)	Hindered (against)

When you have enough answers, explain the word *responsibility*. On the board, show the following definition: "to do your job well enough that you help the group accomplish its job." Ask the students to explain why being responsible was part of making the group and all the class machines work.

Closure

Have the machine groups reform and discuss what they can do differently to be more responsible for a successful run. Watch a demo from each group.

Follow-up

Obtain a copy of *Playfair* or *Learning Through Noncompetitive Activities and Play* (see p. 121). Select cooperative games appropriate to the physical space that you have available. (If there is little space in your classroom, take the class to the playground, gym, lunchroom, or some other open area that will not disturb other classes.) Set the game up so you can adapt the discussion and closure in this lesson to it.

Class Jobs

Materials

index cards, newsprint, marker

Set

On the board or overhead, show a list of classroom jobs. Following is a suggested list, which you may adapt to your room:

- line leader (one per row of desks)
- pick-up captain
- office messenger
- attendance checker
- cage cleaner
- animal feeder
- shelf arranger
- announcement reader
- chief welcomer of guests
- gym team leader (4 students)
- six-inch voice checker
- lunch table leader (6 students)
- chief friend
- cheerleading captain

Do a choral reading with the class. Explain to the class that the classroom is like a machine. To make it run smoothly every part must do its job.

Objective

Tell the students that in this lesson they are going to work on job responsibility for the classroom.

Lesson

1. Put each job on an index card with that job's responsibilities on the back. Invite each child to pick a job card from the pile. Tell them to turn to a partner and read the title on the front of the card and the duties on the back.

| Cheerleading Captain | • Says:
    "Good job!"
    "You can do it!"
• Gives pats on the back.
• Smiles. |

2. Invite everyone to look around and be sure that anyone who needs help reading the card gets it. Ask the children to explain in their own words what their responsibilities are.
3. Explain that they will all keep their jobs for a week and then they will change jobs.
4. Collect the jobs and post them on a name/job chart for all to see.

NAME/JOB CHART

Elisha	animal feeder
David	lunch table leader
Jenny	line leader
Jose	chief friend

If children forget their jobs, they should check the name/job chart.

Discussion

At the end of the day, ask all children to review what they did for their jobs. Put a rating scale (1-10) on the board and invite each child to rate how well he or she took responsibility for the job.

Closure

At the end of the week, ask the children to rate their individual work done that week and to explain why they gave themselves those ratings. After all have shared, give each child an index card with your rating and your reasons for the rating. Concentrate on giving encouragement and cuing to those children who have the most difficulty explaining the self-ratings.

Follow-up

Each week, rotate the jobs. End the week with the self-ratings and feedback. Send a note home to parents with an explanation of this project. Encourage parents to have children select a home job (if not being done already) and use the same self-rating chart. Ask the parents to also offer positive feedback. Encourage the children to bring in their self-ratings for home responsibility. At least once a week, have the children self-rate the role assignments they have in small- group tasks, for example, reader, recorder, encourager.

Lesson 3

Responsibility Web

Materials

overhead (p. 91), worksheet (p. 102), newsprint, pencils, markers, tape

Set

Ask for members of the class to tell you how they show responsibility at home. Give examples such as doing the dishes or helping with the ironing. Give the children about thirty seconds to think and then use a wraparound that starts with a volunteer.

Objective

Explain to the class that they are going to make a list of the most important ways that they can be responsible at school.

Lesson

1. On the board or overhead, make a web (or use master on p. 91).

2. Write *responsibility at school* in the center of the web. Ask some of the children to review what they said during the Set activity. After you have three or four examples, invite the children to think of ways that they act responsibly at school. You want to elicit actions and behaviors. The action should say, "I am a responsible person because I did this." On the web's rays, record the answers that correctly show responsibility at school. If an answer is not "correct" (e.g., it is a home responsibility), affirm the responsibility but indicate that it is one that doesn't apply to school. Ask for another try from the same child.

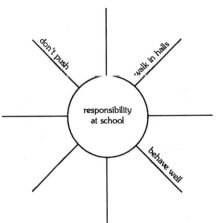

3. After you have gathered all the possibilities on the rays, have children form groups of three. Give a worksheet (see p. 102 for master) and pencil to each group of three. Each group should select one member to record, one to check, and one to encourage. The checker will make sure that all agree on the answers and that all members can explain why the selections were made.

RESPONSIBILITY WORKSHEET

1. From the web on the board, pick the three responsibilities that are most important for a student in this classroom. List the choices you all agree on here.

    a.

    b.

    c.

2. After you all agree and each of you can explain why these three are most important, sign your names somewhere on this sheet.

4. Review the instructions with the groups. Check for understanding. When all are ready, begin the task.

5. After five minutes, signal the students to stop, look, and listen. Ask each group's recorder to read the choices made by its group. On the class web, star or check each idea mentioned. Ask every third recorder to explain why the group made a choice. You may want to alter who in the group explains a choice. Compliment responses.

6. After all the choices are given, tally the responses on the web. Make a list of the three most popular items (most stars or checks) and read them with the class.

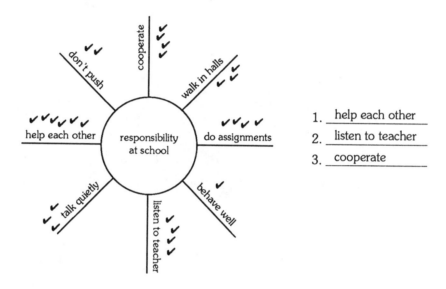

1. <u>help each other</u>
2. <u>listen to teacher</u>
3. <u>cooperate</u>

Discussion

Ask the children how they think they have been doing with these items in the classroom: Very well? OK? Not yet perfected? Encourage the students to give reasons for their answers.

Closure

In the groups of three, invite each child to share one of the top three school responsibilities he or she could improve upon. Encourage the group members to listen to each other and to remember what is said so they can help each other throughout the day. Post the top three school responsibilities for all to see and review.

Follow-up

Repeat this lesson with discussion and closure, but change the focus from "responsibilities at school" to "responsibilities at home," "responsibilities when visiting a friend's house," or something else.

Lesson
4

Responsibility Goals

Materials

"Score Your Goal" overhead (p. 92), "Goal Scoreboard" overhead (p. 93), index cards, colored dots or markers

Set

Show the "Score your goal" overhead. Ask the children to share what they think it means to score a goal. Ask the students to name some sports in which goals are scored. Ask how it feels to score a goal.

Objective

Explain to the children that in this lesson they are going to score goals in a responsibility game.

Lesson

1. On the goal overhead, write the words *responsibility in school*. Use a choral reading to review the chart of the top three school responsibilities in the last lesson.

2. Invite the children to form groups of three. In each group you will want a strong reader, an average reader, and a reader who may

need a little more practice. You can do this by dividing your class list into thirds. One-third of the list should be your best readers, one-third the average, and one-third the ones who may need more practice. Use three-by-five index cards. Each card should have a colored dot on it: red for the strong readers, blue for the middle readers, and yellow for the ones needing more practice. Give the cards out alphabetically. As soon as all cards are in the children's hands, tell them to find two partners with different colored dots. Each group of three needs to have three different colors in it. Do not say anything about the color selection process.

3. In the groups, each child will greet each other and say, "Glad to be with you," as they shake hands in greeting.

4. Instruct each child to select one of the top three school responsibilities to make into a goal chart and read to the group. All members should help each other with the reading task.

5. When all have read the selections in the group, the yellow dot is to get three worksheets (p. 92) from you and give one to each group member.

SCORE YOUR GOAL WORKSHEET (sample)

6. Instruct the students to write their names on the player on the worksheet. On the ball, have them write one or two words for the item selected from the top three school responsibilities. On the net, have them write the words *my responsibility*.

7. After the students have completed their worksheets, each student will tell its group why he or she thinks it is important to do the responsibility written on the ball.

Discussion

When the groups finish the roundrobin sharing, take each item from the list of the top three and ask the children to complete this sentence (for each of the three items): "Doing (item) in class is a good idea because_____." As the ideas are shared, list them on the board. Remember to encourage and cue the children with the yellow dots as much as the others, if not more.

Closure

Invite the children to individually keep count through the day of how many times they score a goal by doing one of the top three behaviors. Whenever the students score, they should remember to mark the score on their worksheets. At the end of the day, the groups will get back together to count up the scores and see how they did as a team. (Don't forget to allow time for this.) Pass out copies of the Goal Scoreboard (see p. 93) to record their scores. Note: It is better if the students stay in this group for at least a week. Each day, give the groups five minutes at the start of the day to review the day's responsibility goal and five minutes at the end of the day to record the scores and discuss what they did.

GOAL SCOREBOARD (sample)

Name	Talk Quietly	Cooperate	Help Each Other	Listen to Teacher	Score Total
Joe	✓✓	✓	✓	✓	5
Sally	✓	--	✓	✓	3
Jennifer	--	✓✓	✓✓✓	✓	6
Maria	✓✓	✓✓	✓✓	✓	7
Bob	✓	✓	--	✓	3

Follow-up

Adapt the scoring system to a different focus, such as responsibility at home, responsibility at a friend's house, etc. Carry each lesson through the discussion and closure.

Lesson 5

Team Responsibility

Materials

"Score Your Goal" worksheets (p. 92), "Goal Scoreboard" worksheets (p. 93), newsprint, markers, tape, index cards, colored dots

Set

Put the children into the same groups of three used to make the responsibility goal sheets (see previous lesson). Invite them to add up the daily scores for each member. After they have helped each other with this and checked their answers, help them tabulate the team total. (If you do this lesson after only one day's scoring, then you will only need a team total. It is better if they have three to five days of scores to use.)

Ask each child with a blue dot to call out his or her team's total. Divide the total by the number of days tallied and give the group its average score (round off all numbers). For example: the student says, "Our team total is twelve." The teacher says, "You worked four days. Your base score is three."

Objective

Explain to the children that they are going to see how teamwork can help them accomplish their individual goals.

Lesson

1. With the same trios, have each student select a different number from one to ten. The low number will record the group's answers; the high number will encourage the group while working; the middle number will check for agreement in the group for its answers. (Put the responsibilities on the board for reference.)

2. Invite each group member to think of a name for its group. From those nominations, the group must agree on a name for the group.

3. Once the group has agreed on its name, the encourager will get a large sheet of newsprint and a box of crayons or markers from the materials table. The group will use the materials to sketch three players (stick figures are OK), a large ball, and a net for a game of choice. As they did on the individual sheets, they will name the players, write the chosen responsibilities on the ball and write the words *our responsibilities* on the net. (Show a sample on the overhead.) In the first quarter box of the scoreboard, they will enter this team's average score earned (see the set activity).

4. Explain that for the rest of the day, they will work on their individual goals for responsibility. At the end of the day, the group will get together to add up the team score and enter it into the box. On the following days, they will add new daily scores. At the end of the week, they will add up the week's score.

5. Each day, allow time for teams to total the scores. To check on the entries, take a few minutes to allow the children to share in the groups or with the whole class what they did to earn the points.

Discussion

At the end of the week, total all scores for the week in the final score box. Ask how many teams had higher daily scores at the end of the week than at the beginning of the week. (Encourage students to explain the change.)

Closure

Ask students to tell how they helped each other and how it felt to work together as a team. Invite them to ask each other, "What did we do well?" "What could we do differently next time?"

Follow-up

Adapt lessons from *Playfair* or *Learning Through Noncompetitive Activities and Play* (see p. 121) for team games. Refer to *Start Them Thinking* (see p. 120) for cooperative learning activities. Use the instructions, discussion, and closure from this lesson to focus follow-up lessons on team responsibility.

WORKING TOGETHER

Working together is a norm that is important for students who will graduate in the next century. Whether they work as a manager for a company such as GE, Hewlett Packard, or DuPont, or as a hospital doctor or nurse, or as an athlete on a team, they will need to know how to work together or cooperate. In this unit, you will introduce them to the importance of working together.

Getting Together

Materials

cartoon strips cut into thirds (p. 103), glue, scissors, newsprint, crayons or markers, cut-out figures of squares, triangles, and circles

Set

Cut cartoon strips into thirds, and randomly give each student a piece. As soon as each student has a piece, everyone is to find the other two matching pieces and sit down with those students. As soon as all trios are seated, ask volunteers to tell you how they helped each other get a whole strip. Write *working together* and *cooperating* on the board and help the students pronounce each with choral reading practice. Show the pictures on the overhead.

Objective

Explain to the students that in today's lesson they are going to explore the idea of working together or cooperating.

Lesson

1. Make a double T-chart for working together/cooperating. Ask students to help fill in the chart by building on what they have learned about cooperating in earlier lessons or in putting together the cartoon strips.

WORKING TOGETHER/COOPERATION		
LOOKS LIKE	SOUNDS LIKE	FEELS LIKE

2. Give each group a sheet of newsprint, two or three crayons or markers, a tub of paste or glue, and a set of three of each of cut-out figures (squares, triangles, circles). Make the cut-outs three different colors in each set.

3. First, have each child in a group select one color. Assign one color to designate the designer. The designer lays out the cut-outs in the pattern the group agrees upon. The next color determines the paster. The paster applies the paste and presses the pieces in place. The last color is the encourager and checker. This person makes sure all members in the trio agree on a pattern and place for each piece. The checker will also report to the class about the finished design.

4. The team may decide to decorate the newsprint or the pieces in any way the members agree. Allow ten to fifteen minutes for the work.

5. When a team finishes, all members can sign the completed sheet and give the final work a name.

Discussion

Invite each checker to describe in turn the group's completed work. The other members will hold it up for all to see. After the work is described, each member will share one thing he or she did that showed cooperation. Lead a special hurrah as each group finishes.

Closure

Invite each group to invent a group name for itself. The name should tell something about the cooperation of the group. Do a group wraparound to share the names.

Follow-up

Try this lesson with new groups of three, this time using paint, clay, or some other art medium. Lead the group in the same Discussion and Closure exercises as above.

Cooperation at the Circus

Materials

"Circus!" video (see p. 117) or an appropriate story that you read, video recorder, television monitor

Set

Ask the class, "How many have been to a circus? How many have seen a circus on television? How many have a favorite character at the circus?" Let them raise their hands for each answer. After the last question, ask individuals, "Who is your favorite character? Why?"

Objective

Explain to the children that this lesson will focus on cooperation at the circus.

Lesson

1. Invite every child to pick a partner. Be sure everyone has a partner (no more than one threesome).

2. Use the overhead or board to read the question, "Why do you think cooperation is important to make the circus a success?" Invite the partners to discuss and agree on an answer.

3. After a few minutes, sample a variety of responses. Write them on the board. When you have all the possibilities the pairs can think of, do a guided choral reading of the list with the class. Compliment their good thinking and then invite them to watch the video "Circus" (or read them an appropriate story). Invite them to see how many ideas from the list are shown in the video.

4. After the video or story, invite the same partners to agree on at least one idea from the video that was on the class list.

5. Invite a random number of pairs to share the idea they picked and to tell why they picked it.

Discussion

On the board or overhead, put the stem, "Working together in the circus is important because...." Have the partners share ideas. Next, sample the ideas and compliment the contributions. Be sure to cue the hesitant pairs.

Closure

Invite the partners to shake hands and say to each other, "Thanks for helping me with your good ideas."

Follow-up

Allow time for children to create a class circus that shows cooperation. Let the students draw a class mural on a banner or large piece of paper, or combine individuals' posters to make a large mural, or pass out clay for each person to sculpt a part of the class circus.

Lesson 3

Our Circus

Materials

job cards (p. 104–106), costumes or props, circus music and player (tape or record), newsprint, crayons

Set

Ask the children to remember how the circus people worked together. Invite several students to share what they recall.

Objective

Explain to the children that today they are going to start a circus project to practice working together.

Lesson

1. Review the Working Together/Cooperation double T-chart from Lesson 1 of this unit with a choral reading.
2. Distribute to each child a circus job card. (See p. 104–106 for job cards.)

- trapeze artist (3)
- lion tamer (1)
- lion (3)
- assistant lion tamer (2)
- elephant (3)
- elephant trainer
- elephant roust-a-bout (2)
- clown (3)
- horseback rider (3)
- horse (3)
- ringmaster
- band leader
- band member (4)
- puppeteer (3)

3. Instruct cardholders to find others that fit in their team (trapeze artists, horses, lions and lion tamers, etc.). Have all sit with their team and read their job cards. Only if no one in a team can read the card may the cardholder ask you for help.

4. Give the groups about ten to fifteen minutes to plan what they are going to do to show how they must work together at the circus. They will have a chance to show the class by acting out the plan. Encourage them to bring costumes and props from home. (Break here.)

5. Allow another ten minutes for the groups to get ready for their presentations. Set the desks in a circle so that you have a ring and an audience. Add some circus music if you are able. Encourage those students not in the ring to be the audience and applaud after each act. Start and end with the ringmaster.

Discussion

Invite each team in turn to share how it felt to work together. Make a list of the "feeling" words for a choral reading.

Closure

Give each circus team a piece of newsprint and crayons. Have the teams sketch a picture of itself as a circus team working together. Each should sign the completed work before you post it.

Follow-up

Allow the children other opportunities to do this lesson, but change the focus to a zoo, construction site, television show, or something similar. Remember to discuss how they felt cooperating and allow time for them to sketch what they did.

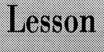

Lesson 4

Puppet Performance

Materials

cut-out puppets (p. 107 & 108), glue, crayons or markers, scraps of material, newsprint, tape, bulletin board

Set

Move the children into the teams that they had in the previous lesson. Have them identify in each team the person who woke earliest that morning and designate that person to be the materials manager. Invite the materials managers to get a set of puppet materials from the materials table. These materials include a set of the puppet cut-outs, crayons or markers, and scraps of material.

Objective

Explain to the children that they are going to make puppet shows that show how to work together in school.

Lesson

1. Allow five minutes for everyone on a team to name one of the puppets and have a chance to suggest an idea for the story. The

story will take place in the Washington Carver Primary School. It will show how students can work together on a school task (reading a story or cleaning up the blocks, for example). If helpful, brainstorm with the whole class a list of ideas for stories. Write the list on the board.

2. Allow ten minutes for the children to decorate their puppets.

3. Allow ten minutes for the team to practice its story.

4. The student sitting to the right of the materials manager will tell the story to the audience before the group's performance. The third student in the group will ask the audience after the performance to tell why it was important for the puppets to work together.

Discussion

Invite each of the teams to discuss what they learned about working together from the other performances. Tape several dialogue balloons on the board. In the dialogue balloons, write what each group says they learned that day.

Closure

Ask each person to sign his or her puppet. Post the puppets on a giant bulletin board titled "Working Together in School." Attach the cartoon dialogue balloons to show which ideas were learned by each group.

Follow-up

Schedule the teams to present the shows to other classes, senior citizens, or parents.

Lesson
5

Story Performance

Materials

stories for groups to read (Aesop's Fables, Grimm, and Mother Goose provide lots of easy reader examples), eight-by-eleven-inch index cards, markers, newsprint, crayons

Set

Ask student volunteers to read the list of stories. After a title is read by a volunteer, lead a choral reading of it.

Objective

Explain to the children that they are going practice working together on a school task.

Lesson

1. Form new groups of five. In each group have one student who can read.

2. Have the reader select a story he or she can read. Make sure that the stories you provide have at least four roles. The reader will read to the rest of group. When the story is done, the group will work

together to make sure all can retell the story, at least in an abbreviated manner.

3. Give the person sitting to the right of the reader five index cards. This person is the writer. The group will agree on the five roles it will play so that it can present the story to the class. With as much help as needed from the rest of the group and the book, the writer will put one character's name on a card. If there are not five characters, one card may be an important object in the story. For example, in the "Three Billy Goats Gruff" the roles would be the largest brother, the medium brother, the little brother, the troll, and the bridge.

4. Give the groups time to plan and rehearse the plays. Everyone will have a role to play. Let them know that before each play you will select one member of the group to tell the story the class will see. Provide markers and blank eight-by-eleven-inch cards so that the group may invent and label props. Encourage them to use words from the book for any labels they make (bridge, meadow, or troll, for example).

5. Allow the groups to present their plays in turn. Begin each play by asking one member to tell the story.

6. After the play, encourage hurrahs and elicit comments from the audience, such as, "That is a wonderful story because..." Select one member of the performing group to tell you one way the team worked well together. Make a list on the board with the different ideas.

Discussion

After the last presentation, discuss how working together was important when they worked in reading groups. What were some of the most helpful things they did together?

Closure

Give each group a sheet of newsprint and crayons. Have them create an advertisement for their play. The ad should include pictures, the names of the cast members and a title for the play. Hang the ads up for all to see.

Follow-up

Use this reading/acting lesson in other subject areas. Have students act out math problems, how a plant grows, a historical event, a poem, or something else the class is studying. One member can read the study unit or instructions. The group can then create the props and practice their performance.

PROBLEM SOLVING

In the past two decades, school curricula have moved more and more to facts, recall, and regurgitation. Much of this movement, forced by the legislative cries for accountability and the inability and unwillingness of the testing industry to move beyond a narrow focus on the highly reliable measurement of bits of information and low-order basic microskills, has left a nation of students whose problem-solving capabilities have become greatly weakened. Unfortunately, this has occurred at a time when the demand for problem-solving skills in all areas of education, science, law, government, business, and industry throughout the world has increased. With this increased pressure and the advances in the cognitive sciences, which have provided new insights into the nature of learning, a technology of problem solving has emerged for use throughout the school curricula.

While there are people who would prefer that school children not face the word *problem* (they see only its negative overtones), we take the position that one of the best ways to help children exercise their social responsibility is to teach them the language, the skills, and the strategies of problem solving. This means that they will have to learn to pinpoint blocks, barriers, and obstacles to the improvement of society and label them as "problems." It will also mean that they will need to take command of the strategies for solving those problems, not only as individual entrepreneurs, but also as responsible members of society. Knowledge of the technology of problem solving is not enough. That is why, in these lessons designed to introduce primary students to problem solving, we have structured tasks that enable them to experience, practice, and develop their basic problem-solving skills.

In past generations, it may have been sufficient for children to gather information, commit it to memory and pass a fact-based test. In today's high-tech world, the information explosion makes it impossible for even the best memories to absorb every bit of information. Thus, it is important that today's young students begin early to learn how to control information and to put it to the best uses for themselves and the society of which they are a responsible part.

Lesson 1

What's The Problem?

Materials

overhead (p. 94), "Nate the Great and the Sticky Case" video (see p. 117), TV, video recorder, index cards, colored dots or markers, role cards, tacks for bulletin board, "Nate's Problem" worksheets (see p. 109 & 110), newsprint, tape

Set

Show the "worried boy" overhead (p. 94) . Ask the children to tell you why they think the boy is worried. Take many answers and then help them focus on the idea that he is trying to solve a problem.

Objective

Explain to the class that today's lesson will focus on solving problems.

Lesson

1. Ask the children to share with you what they think problems are. Write the answers down for all to see. Point out the ideas that are closest to the idea of a problem as a special challenge, a barrier or block, or something that is hard to do. Use the overhead from the

Set activity to illustrate. Add other examples familiar to your students and their cultures.

2. Tell the students that they are going to see a video about how a young boy, Nate, had to find an answer or solution to a difficult question. Tell them to watch for what that special problem was, what the answer was and most importantly, how Nate solved the problem. If you are unable to show a video, substitute an appropriate story.

3. After the video or story, put the children into new groups of three. Use cards with colored dots to assign teams. Change which colors are given to each job. The red dots will be the recorder, the yellow the checker, and the blue the encourager. The checkers will check for agreement and the ability of each member to explain the group's final answer. Ask the recorders to pick up a "Nate's Problem" worksheet (p. 109) and a large sheet of newsprint for their group. Explain that they will write their group answers to the questions on the newsprint. Model the chart for them on the board or overhead (see Chart 2).

Chart 1
NATE'S PROBLEM WORKSHEET

1. Agree on each answer.
2. Put the answer in the square with the matching letter.
    a. What do you agree was Nate's problem?
    b. What do you agree was his solution?
    c. What personal talents did Nate use to solve the problem.?
    d. What do you agree was Nate's best talent?
    e. Agree on one different way you think Nate might have solved the problem.

---

4. When all answers are recorded and all agree, each group member should sign the group sheet. While waiting for other groups to finish, the early birds should check to see that all can explain the answers with a roundrobin quiz.

Discussion

Ask the questions listed on the worksheet. Identify students with a different colored dot in each group to share the answers. For each block, invite three or four different groups to answer. Remind the class that you're asking for answers that their group agreed upon. As you proceed from block to block, record single cue words on the board. Invite the students to listen for ideas they did not have in their own groups. Avoid calling on groups a second time until every group has had a chance to share ideas on at least one question. This way you can assure a more equal distribution of responses.

Closure

Give each group a copy of Chart 2 (p. 110). Instruct the red dots to agree on the proper title of each block. After they have the order the group agrees is correct, have them pick words from the appropriate blocks on the board and put them in place. Give a demonstration. When the groups are finished, each member should sign the group sheet. Collect these.

Chart 2 (sample)	
a. the problem	b. the solution
c. his talents	d. his best talent
e. another solution	f. your signatures

Follow-up

Adapt the primary lesson, discussion, and closure to other stories. Refer to the video appendix (p. 117) or select and read stories appropriate to your children. If you have a sufficient number of strong readers to put one in every group of three, structure your adaptation of the "Nate" lesson to allow for the student readers. It is very important that you encourage the repetitious use of the blocks and the focus on problem solving when the students are discussing the stories.

Score

Materials

wastebasket, crumpled paper, chalk

Set

Young students see many games on TV...basketball, hockey, football. By now they know the object of most games is to score. Baskets, goals, and touchdowns are common terms to them. Ask the class to brainstorm all the sports in which scoring points is important. List the sport and the way a player gets points (e.g., touchdown).

Objective

Explain to the children that they are going to examine different ways to set goals. Explain the connection between a goal in a game (e.g., touchdown, basket) and a life goal (something we want).

Lesson

1. Place a wastebasket on a chair. On the floor, in front of the basket, mark two-foot lines with the scores.

2. Divide the class into four teams. Each team will have three minutes to get the highest score it can. All members must have a chance to shoot from one of the numbered squares.

3. Give each team three minutes to agree on a strategy. Points are scored by a "basket" x the box total. One shot scored from 4=4. Five shots from 3=15. Have a box of crumpled 8 1/2" x 11" paper ready for each round.

4. Total points on the board after each round for each team. Highest total wins.

Discussion

Ask each team to explain and judge its strategy in relation to its goal. Discuss what they would do differently the next time.

Closure

Each team will discuss and share this idea. "Scoring points in this game is like goal setting in life because _____."

Follow-up

Each day for the next two weeks, allow the same teams to improve on their previous day's performance. Give three minutes to plan strategy beforehand and three minutes to evaluate after. At the end of the week, ask teams to explain in their own words the difference between a "strategy" and a "goal."

Lesson 3

The Magic Robot

Materials

Robot overhead (p. 95), problem-solving observation chart (p. 96), index cards

Set

Show the robot overhead. Ask the children to share with the class all they know about robots. Make a list on the board.

Objective

Explain that in this lesson, they are going to be given a number of different problems to solve, and that they will solve them by inventing different robots.

Lesson

1. Divide the class into groups of five to seven. Remind them that everyone on the team needs the chance to contribute ideas and to be a part of the robot.

2. Review the problem-solving observation chart (see p. 96). Let them know that you will use it to see how well they use the behaviors as they solve the problems you will give.

3. Explain that you are going to present a problem. Each group will have a few minutes to create a robot that will solve the problem. When all are ready, each group will demonstrate how its robot works.

4. Share the first problem: "Once upon a time, there was a little girl who fell very ill. She was so ill, she could not go to school or play with her friends. She could only wish that she had some machine in her room that would make her happy." Instruct the teams to make a machine that will grant her wish.

5. Monitor the teams and note on your chart what problem-solving behaviors they use.

6. Invite each team to demonstrate its robot. After each robot is demonstrated, select one member of each team to explain what its robot did and why. Select a second team member to tell what the team did well in solving the problem. Add any positive feedback you have for the team's problem solving.

7. After all teams have finished, invite the teams to discuss among its members how they might do better in the next round as problem solvers.

8. On the next day, share another problem: "Once upon a time, there was a little boy who wanted a very special birthday gift. The problem was that you could only find this gift, which weighed one thousand pounds, in a country on the other side of the world." Instruct the teams to make a robot that will deliver the present to the boy's home. Repeat steps 6 and 7 above.

9. On as many following days as you wish, share a problem that the teams can solve by making a robot. You may keep the same teams or you may mix them differently each day. Follow steps 6 and 7.

Discussion

After you feel the children have practiced enough, put a one-to-ten rating scale on the board. Ask each child to rate how he or she has improved as a problem solver. After a few moments, invite five to seven volunteers to share the self-ratings and why they gave themselves those ratings. Listen attentively and thank each volunteer.

Closure

Give each team an index card. Invite the teams to agree on a rating for the whole team as problem solvers. When they reach agreement, the members should sign the team card and turn it in to you. After you have collected all the cards, praise the class for the specific improvements you have noted. Use the chart for visual reinforcement.

Follow-Up

Have each team make up a problem that a special robot could solve. You can rotate the problems among the teams so that each team solves another team's problems, each team solves the problem it created, or all the teams solve one problem at a time on successive days. Although making the robot will be fun, it is most important that you keep the children's focus on the problem solving that they are doing. This is done by your constant referral to the chart and completion of steps six and seven after each lesson.

Make A Story

Materials

index cards, colored dots or markers, copies of scenarios (p. 111), problem-solving worksheet (p. 112), sequence chart (p. 113), optional props

Set

Ask the children to help you make a list of their favorite television shows. Put the list on the board and invite the children to share why they picked those shows.

Objective

Explain to the children that today's lesson will focus on how to make a story that shows a problem being solved.

Lesson

1. Divide the class into groups of three. Use the dots to determine the reader, the checker, and the encourager.

2. Give each group a scenario to read. Help with any reading that the group members cannot do. Let them know that they are to discuss

the situation, decide who will play what role, agree upon how they will solve the problem, and practice the play.

THE SCENARIOS

"Mary is a new girl in the school. She has no friends. On the playground she is standing all by herself." Your group sees her. Decide how you can help her make friends. Make a play without words to show this.

_____

"Juan has lost his milk money for lunch." Decide what you can do to help him. Make a play without words to show this.

_____

"Sue Ellen forgot to bring a note from home to go on the field trip." Decide what you can do to help her. Make a play without words to show this.

_____

"Carl was in fight on the bus with a bully. He is afraid to get on the bus again." Decide what you can do to help him. Make a play without words to show this.

_____

"Marie was absent for a whole week. She has a lot of math to catch up." Decide what you can do to help her. Make a play without words to show this.

_____

"Margaret's best friend was hurt. The friend fell from her bike and hit her head. The friend is in the hospital." Decide what you can do to help her. Make a play without words to show this.

_____

"Carla's mom forgot to pick her up after school. Your sister is going to pick you and your friends up and drive you home." Decide how you can help her. Make a play without words to show this.

_____

"Jamie lost his new team jacket. He thinks someone stole it." Decide how you can help him. Make a play without words to show this.

_____

"Some big kids said mean things to Kate. They hurt her feelings." Decide how you can help her. Make a play without words to show this.

_____

"Gerry just had a fight with her group. She walked away. She said she never wants to be in that group again." Decide how you can help her. Make a play without words to show this.

_____

"Jo called Tony, her best friend, a bad name." Decide how you can help her make up to Tony. Make a play without words to show this.

_____

"Tom doesn't have any lunch. He is very embarrassed." Decide how you can help him. Make a play without words to show this.

_____

"A gang member wants Ralph to join the gang and deliver crack." Decide how you can help him say no. Make a play without words to show this.

_____

"Robin's friends want her to steal doll clothes at the toy store." Decide how you can help her say no. Make a play without words to show this.

3. You can decide whether you want the students to have props or not. Once the groups have practiced the plays, do a roundrobin of presentations. After each play, ask the actors to explain why they selected the solution they presented. Give each group of performers a round of applause after the discussion.

Discussion

Display the problem-solving worksheet (p. 112) for all to see. Ask for volunteers to tell which of the problem-solving behaviors were used in deciding how to help.

Closure

Give each group a copy of the following sequence chart (p. 113). Ask them to fill in each of the blocks with one or two words. When all agree on the answers, each group member will sign the chart and hand it in to you.

SEQUENCE CHART

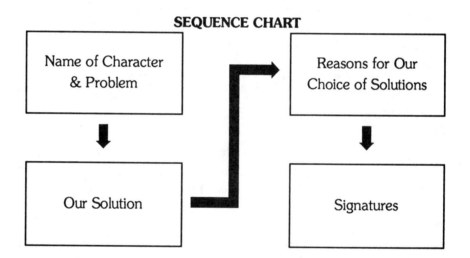

Follow-up

Select a short story for each group of three to read. Be sure each group has a reader. After the reader reads to the other children in the group, the group will decide how to act out all or part of the story for the class. One member other than the reader will summarize the story and the third will explain how the group used problem solving in the task. All three will act the selected part. Be sure all groups receive applause.

Lesson 5

Problem-Solving Stories

Materials

problem-solving observation charts (p. 96), selected video (see p. 117), TV, video recorder, index cards, colored dots, problem-solving worksheet (p. 112), masking tape

Set

Post the problem-solving observation chart for the children to review the listed behaviors. Select a strong reader to read each behavior and lead the class in a choral reading review. Indicate that you will use the chart again as you observe them practicing the behaviors during the group work for this lesson.

Objective

Explain to the class that they are going to practice using problem-solving behaviors.

Lesson

1. Select a story on video. (You may use this same lesson outline for several problem-solving practice lessons.) Following is a selection

of story videos (see also p. 117). Be sure to preview each one to determine the spots in the story where you want to stop and have the students discuss the questions. (You may wish to substitute a story that you read to the class. Use the same questions at the appropriate spot in each story. If you have sufficient readers, before the video or in place of the video, have a reader in each group read the story and stop at the places you indicate so that the groups can discuss the questions.)

- The Tinder Box
- The Emperor's New Clothes
- The Staunch Tin Soldier
- Sleeping Beauty
- Little Tom Thumb
- The Frog Prince
- Tale of the Ugly Duckling
- Hansel and Gretel
- Rumpelstiltskin
- The Boy Who Cried Wolf
- The Ears of King Midas

2. Before you start the video, divide the class into groups of three. Use cards with colored dots to determine the jobs in each group. The reader will read the questions and the story, if you elect that approach. The recorder will write the answers. The checker will make sure that all members agree to each answer.

3. Give a copy of the problem-solving worksheet (p. 112) to each recorder:

NAMES		
THE PROBLEM	WAYS TO SOLVE THE PROBLEM	THE SOLUTION

4. Tell the children that you will stop the video as soon as the problem or challenge is identified. Review the questions on the problem-solving observation chart that the group will use at this spot. After you have shown the video or told the story, allow five minutes for each group to fill in the first block on their problem-solving worksheet, "the problem."

5. Repeat the procedure for each of the remaining two blocks. Tell where you will stop, review the appropriate problem-solving behaviors, and allow five minutes after the video.

Discussion

Ask for sample responses to each of the blocks. Write the samples on the board and discuss the variations. Encourage the class to agree on a single response. Do not suggest or give an answer. Summarize what each group reports and ask for agreements. Finalize the agreement for each block on the chart before you proceed to the next one. When you are gathering the data from the groups, avoid going back to the same groups.

Closure

Invite the groups to write the following on the back of the problem-solving worksheet: (1) a lesson they learned from how the character(s) in this story solved the problem; (2) what problem-solving behaviors from the chart they used well. Sample the responses to each question. After the groups have shared their answers to the second question, use the chart to give your feedback on the problem-solving behaviors you observed. Post it for the class to see.

Follow-up

Chart the children's uses of the problem-solving behaviors so they can see their own progress. You may wish to add an incentive for the class to reach certain milestones. Use of the chart will benefit the students most if you use this same lesson outline with a sequence of stories.

CONFLICT RESOLUTION

Learning how to resolve conflict in a positive way is an advanced, but increasingly necessary social skill for young children to learn. On television, at the movies, and even at home, the models of conflict resolution that children see or experience may focus on verbal if not physical violence. Thus, it ought not be surprising that children often first respond to conflict by hitting, kicking, or lashing out with hurtful, hateful words.

The social skills introduced in previous lessons are important building blocks for learning the more complex skill of conflict resolution. In the early years, we have placed the emphasis on helping children recognize some of the most common forms of conflict they may experience in everyday life (the bully, peer pressure, gang pressure) . We have also helped them see through the mass media and develop a thoughtful response pattern. In this set of lessons, special emphasis is placed on helping children recognize conflict, see its effects, and develop strategies to resolve conflict in constructive ways.

What is Conflict?

Materials

string, paste tubs, blunt scissors, poster board, crayons, newsprint, old magazines, masking tape, collage instructions (p. 97)

Set

Divide the children into pairs. Invite the pairs to sit on the floor facing each other. Give each pair a twelve-inch piece of string. Have each partner grab an end of the string. At your signal, each partner will pull the string as hard as possible. Stop the pull after 30 seconds and invite the partners to shake hands.

Objective

On the board write the word *conflict* and explain to the children that today they are going to learn about this word.

Lesson

1. On the board or a large piece of newsprint, trace a double T-chart entitled "Conflict."

CONFLICT

LOOKS LIKE	SOUNDS LIKE	FEELS LIKE

2. Ask the children to give you specific words to describe what conflict looked like, sounded like, or felt like when they were pulling on the strings. List the words they give with as little elaboration as possible under the appropriate headings on the double T-chart. If the children have difficulty phrasing the behaviors and feelings, cue them with such questions as "Do you think it looked like _____?" "What else did conflict look like?" Seek responses from many different class members.

3. Review the chart with a guided choral reading to help all with the correct pronunciation of the words.

4. Divide the class into pairs, the same pairs or new ones.

5. Review your class guidelines for behavior in group work with a choral reading of your posted guidelines as used in Unit 1.

6. Assign a role to each child in each pair. You will need materials managers and pasters. The materials manager will get the materials, see that they are organized, and return them to the materials table when the task is done. The paster will paste the collage pictures on the cardboard. Both children will select and take turns cutting the pictures for the collage.

7. Invite the materials managers to get scissors, a tub of paste, a piece of poster board (at least 12 by 18 inches) and several magazines from the materials table.

8. Use an overhead or the board to list the following task instructions for making a collage. Show them a completed collage with examples of conflict pictures.

9. Review the steps with a choral reading. Check for understanding of each step.

10. Monitor and assist the groups. Give positive feedback at each step.

11. When the groups are done, monitor the return of materials and post the completed work. (This is a good spot for a break.) End the task with praise to the class for what they did well.

12. (Begin the next day.) Post a new double T-chart and label it "Working Together." Indicate that this is the opposite of the "Conflict" double T-chart. As above, invite the class to fill in the chart with things they said, did, or felt as they worked together on the conflict collage.

13. Over the next few days, spend five to ten minutes allowing each group to show its collage. Encourage each group to share what it likes about its collage. Give positive feedback and a class hurrah to each pair.

CONFLICT COLLAGE INSTRUCTIONS

1. Find pictures that show people in conflict.

2. Take turns cutting out the pictures.

3. Give each other encouragement. Say, for example, "That's a great picture!"

4. Agree on your arrangement.

5. Pasters put the paste on the pictures.

6. Materials managers put the pictures on the board. Both partners agree on the spots.

7. Sign your names when done.

8. Clean up and have the materials managers put the materials back.

Discussion

After all the sharing is done, hold an all-class discussion on what the children have learned about conflict. Use the following to wrap around the class for answers: "About conflict, I learned...." As each student makes a statement (some may say, "I pass"), record it on the board. At the end of the wraparound, summarize their ideas.

Closure

Invite the children to shake hands with each of the persons around them and say, "Thanks for helping with this lesson."

Follow-up

Invite the children to find other visual examples of conflict in magazines, television, movies, or other media. Structure the task so that they can build on the ideas presented in the above lesson.

Lesson 2

Conflict Blocks

Materials

"block definitions" overhead (p. 98), wooden blocks, tickets

Set

Distribute one wooden block to each child. Draw a line on the floor across the middle of the classroom. Invite the students one by one to use the blocks to build a wall across the classroom. When the wall is done, place half the class on each side of the wall.

Objective

Explain to the class that today they are going to learn how conflict blocks or hinders work getting done in the classroom.

Lesson

1. Distribute one half of a ticket to each child in the room. Be sure that some of the tickets are split across the wall. After all tickets are distributed, tell the students that they must find the matching half.

They may not cross the wall to find the matching half. If the missing half is on the other side of the wall, it must stay there. Allow three to five minutes for matching their tickets. When a match is made, the partners may sit down together on their side of the wall. Unmatched partners must stay standing until you give everyone the signal to stop matching.

2. Ask the students who do not have a match on their own side to tell how it felt being blocked by the wall. List the words on the board.

3. Ask the class to explain the word *block*. Solicit several different definitions before you write on the board or show on the overhead different definitions such as the following:

   a. a solid piece of wood, stone, or metal that has flat sides. (show the wall)

   b. something that gets in the way of doing a task or stops progress or movement (demonstrate an example).

4. Ask the children to give some examples of the ways that conflict can block classroom work (review the conflict double T-chart from the previous lesson). Start with an example that you provide. For example, fighting over a place in line keeps everyone from getting to recess. List the ideas on the board.

5. Discuss one of the conflicts. How does it start? How could it be avoided or changed so as not to block other activities?

6. Take down the block wall and let all pairs find their matching tickets. Tell each pair to select one of the conflicts from the list on the board. Have the pairs agree on how to avoid or change the block.

Discussion

Invite several sample answers from the pairs. Explore the range of different solutions for overcoming or removing the conflict blocks.

Closure

Use a wraparound for the children to complete the sentence, "Conflict is like a wall because..."

Follow-up

Select some situations outside the classroom in which the children may experience conflict (the playground, the lunchroom, the bus, the park, etc.). On different days, repeat steps 4, 5, and 6 and follow up with a discussion and a stem closure. For example, "Today, about conflict, I learned...I discovered...I felt..."

The Hare and the Tortoise

Materials

"The Hare and the Tortoise" video (see p. 117), TV and video recorder (or story), worksheet (p. 114)

Set

Ask the children, "When you are in a race, which do you think is better, to be very fast or to be very steady?" Check for vocabulary understanding and then discuss their ideas.

Objective

Tell the students that in this lesson they are going to explore different ways to solve a conflict.

Lesson

1. Show the video "The Hare and the Tortoise" or read the story.
2. After the story, divide the students into pairs.
3. Designate one student in each pair to be the hare, the other the tortoise.

4. Give the hare a copy of the following worksheet. The hare will record the answers they agree upon.
5. Review the questions before the pairs begin.

THE HARE AND THE TORTOISE
WORKSHEET

a.   What is the conflict in the story?

b.   How was the conflict solved?

c.   Who had the best solution? (Each student give at least one reason.)

1.

2.

3.

Discussion

Ask different tortoises to share the pair's answers to the last question on the worksheet. Seek several different responses and list them on the board or overhead. Ask the class to discuss the reasons and pick the best three by voting.

Closure

Ask each pair to think of a lesson to be learned about conflict from this story. Invite samples.

Follow-up

Select other videos or stories. Adapt the worksheet and the discussion to those stories. Follow the same procedures so that the class comes to agreement on solutions and reasons.

Lesson 4

Bully Up

Materials

"Bully Up: Fighting Feelings" video (see p. 117), TV and video recorder (or story), worksheets (p. 115)

Set

Ask the children what they can do when a bully threatens them. Write the answers on the board for all to see. (The ideas on the board are to be saved for discussion after the movie or story.)

Objective

Tell the children that they are going to study some of the different ways to deal with a bully, other than fighting.

Lesson

1. Show the video, "Bully Up: Fighting Feelings" (or read an appropriate story).
2. After the video or story, match the students into threes. Delegate a recorder, an encourager, and a checker. Review their guidelines for working together and the job of each. The recorder will sketch

the answers from the group. The encourager will make sure that only encouraging remarks are made. The checker will make sure they agree on the answers.

3. Review the worksheet with the groups. For each question, each person in turn should give an answer. After each member has suggested an answer, the trio will agree on the answer to write. They need not worry about spelling.

BULLY UP WORKSHEET

a. What do you think the conflict was in this video?
   Conflict:

b. How does it feel to be pushed around by a bully?
   Feelings:

c. What do you think are better ways to deal with a bully?
   Better Ways:

d. Make a play to show one way to deal with a bully other than fighting. Agree on why you think this is a better way than fighting.
   Because:

4. Encourage as many trios as you have time for to present their plays and explain the choices they made. Give a big hurrah for each presentation.

Discussion

Make a board or overhead list of the various solutions used. Discuss with the entire class the advantages of using these alternatives to fighting with a bully.

Closure

Using the same trios, have each trio agree on some of the ways the members worked together without conflict. Sample the ideas. Compliment the class.

Follow-up

Arrange to have the children show their plays to other classes and explain what they were doing. Have the children make billboard ads for the plays and hang the finished projects in the halls.

Conflict Cartoon

Materials

newsprint or poster board, crayons

Set

Ask the class to brainstorm conflicts that they have outside the classroom. Record the answers on the board or use an overhead of the following chart:

CONFLICT OUTSIDE THE CLASSROOM

With Whom	Where	When	About What

Objective

Explain to the class that in this lesson they will apply all the ideas they have learned about conflict *in* the classroom to conflict *outside* the classroom.

Lesson

1. Divide the class into new groups of three. Give each group a large sheet of newsprint or poster board and a set of crayons.

2. Review the lists on the board. A group may select one item from each column for its conflict story. After the selection, they will sketch or draw (stick figures are OK) a story so that it shows the conflict starting and the conflict ending. For the ending, the group must agree on a method previously discussed in class as OK to use (i.e., other than fighting or hurting others). If you anticipate they will have difficulty remembering good ways to resolve conflicts, take a few moments to brainstorm a review list with the whole class and write the ideas on the board.

3. Each group will decide how to divide the paper into eight parts, how to divide up the tasks so that each person gets an equal chance to draw, and what conflict they will use to make a comic strip.

4. Allow ten to fifteen minutes for the group to make cartoons. When all are finished, each person who contributed will sign the group's cartoon. Post the signed works.

Discussion

Sample the solutions selected by various groups. Ask why the solutions were selected for each conflict.

Closure

Ask each trio to rate itself on a scale of one to ten for how well they settled conflicts in their group while doing the cartoon. Do a wrap-around. Ask one member from each group to give you the rating and others in the same group to say why they selected that number. Encourage all to listen.

Follow-up

Make new groups. Have the new groups select a different conflict for a cartoon. After the new groups make their cartoons, repeat the instructions for the discussion and closure.

OVERHEADS

For your convenience, each overhead is cross-referenced back to the lesson it came from. Look in the lower left-hand corner for the Unit, Lesson and page number.

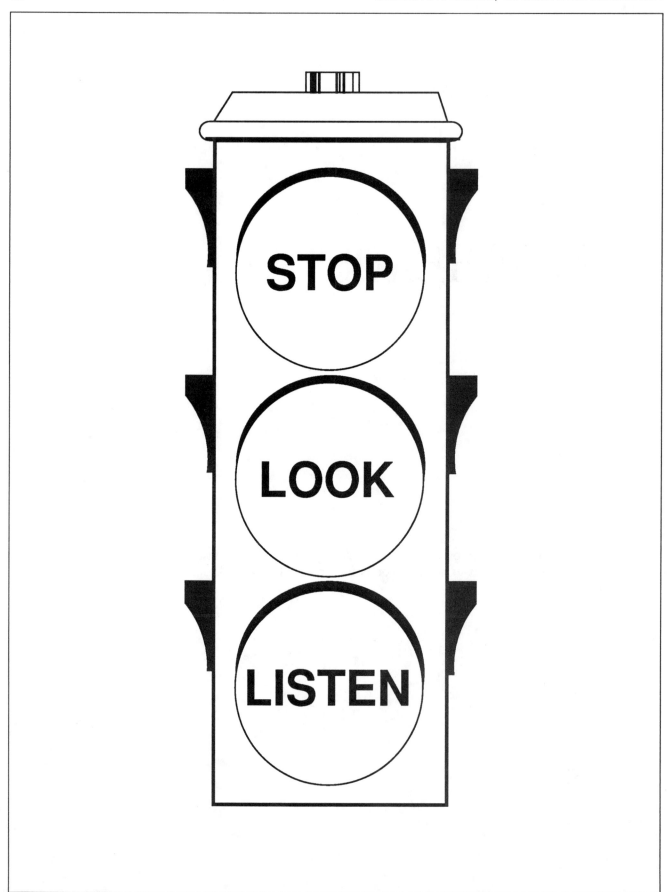

GOOD GROUP MANNERS

- Stay with the group.

- One person talks at a time.

- Use six-inch voices.

- Do your job.

- Use first names.

- Be a cheerleader.

FRIEND OUTLINE

SCORE YOUR GOAL

GOAL SCOREBOARD

Name \ Behavior					

PROBLEM-SOLVING OBSERVATION CHART

What Good Problem Solvers Do and Say	Group or Person
Say: "What is the problem?"	
Say: "How are we sure?"	
Do: Give several reasons for the problem	
Say: "What are ways to solve it?"	
Do: List several ways to solve the problem	
Say: "What is the best way?"	
Do: List several reasons for the choice	

CONFLICT COLLAGE INSTRUCTIONS

1. Find pictures that show people in conflict.

2. Take turns cutting out the pictures.

3. Give each other encouragement. Say, for example, "That's a great picture!"

4. Agree on your arrangement.

5. Pasters put the paste on the pictures.

6. Materials managers put the pictures on the board. Both partners agree on spots.

7. Sign your names when done.

8. Clean up and have the materials managers put the materials back.

DEFINITIONS OF BLOCK

a.   a solid piece of wood, stone, or metal that
     has flat sides.

b.   something that gets in the way of doing a
     task or stops progress or movement.

WORKSHEETS

For your convenience, each worksheet is cross-referenced back to the lesson it came from. Look in the lower left-hand corner for the Unit, Lesson and page number.

Photocopy page on card stock or heavy paper and cut out puppets along dotted lines. Glue or tape sticks to back.

FRIENDSHIP AWARD CERTIFICATE

FRIENDS

_____ is my secret friend!

_____
Friendship behavior

Official Seal Of Friendship

_____
Sign here

◆ Friendship Award Certificate ◆

RESPONSIBILITY WORKSHEET

1. From the web on the board, pick the three responsibilities that are most important for a student in this classroom. List the choices you all agree on here.

   a.

   b.

   c.

2. After you all agree and each of you can explain why these three are most important, sign your names somewhere on this sheet.

Trapeze artist

Lion tamer

Lion

Assistant lion tamer

Elephant

Elephant trainer

Elephant roust-a-bout   **Clown**   **Horseback rider**

Horse   **Ringmaster**   **Band leader**

* Unit 4, Lesson 3, p. 54

Band member   **Band member**   **Puppeteer**

Lion   **Elephant**   **Horse**

Photocopy this page onto card stock or heavy paper. Cut out puppets along dashed lines and glue or tape sticks to back.

Photocopy this page onto card stock or heavy paper. Cut out puppets along dashed lines and glue or tape sticks to back.

NATE'S PROBLEM

Chart 1
Nate's Problem Worksheet

1. Agree on each answer.

2. Put the answer in the square with the matching letter.

    a. What do you agree was Nate's problem?

    b. What do you agree was his solution?

    c. What personal talents did Nate use to solve the problem?

    d. What do you agree was Nate's best talent?

    e. Agree on one different way you think Nate might have solved the problem.

NATE'S PROBLEM

Chart 2	
a.	b.
c.	d.
e.	f.

THE SCENARIOS

"Mary is a new girl in the school. She has no friends. On the playground she is standing all by herself." Your group sees her. Decide how you can help her make friends. Make a play without words to show this.

– –

"Juan has lost his milk money for lunch." Decide what you can do to help him. Make a play without words to show this.

– –

"Sue Ellen forgot to bring a note from home to go on the field trip." Decide what you can do to help her. Make a play without words to show this.

– –

"Carl was in fight on the bus with a bully. He is afraid to get on the bus again." Decide what you can do to help him. Make a play without words to show this.

– –

"Marie was absent for a whole week. She has a lot of math to catch up." Decide what you can do to help her. Make a play without words to show this.

– –

"Margaret's best friend was hurt. The friend fell from her bike and hit her head. The friend is in the hospital." Decide what you can do to help her. Make a play without words to show this.

– –

"Carla's mom forgot to pick her up after school. Your sister is going to pick you and your friends up and drive you home." Decide how you can help her. Make a play without words to show this.

– –

"Jamie lost his new team jacket. He thinks someone stole it." Decide how you can help him. Make a play without words to show this.

– –

"Some big kids said mean things to Kate. They hurt her feelings." Decide how you can help her. Make a play without words to show this.

– –

"Gerry just had a fight with her group. She walked away. She said she never wants to be in that group again." Decide how you can help her. Make a play without words to show this.

– –

"Jo called Tony, her best friend, a bad name." Decide how you can help her make up to Tony. Make a play without words to show this.

– –

"Tom doesn't have any lunch. He is very embarrassed." Decide how you can help him. Make a play without words to show this.

– –

"A gang member wants Ralph to join the gang and deliver crack."
Decide how you can help him say no. Make a play without words to show this.

– –

"Robin's friends want her to steal doll clothes at the toy store." Decide how you can help her say no. Make a play without words to show this.

PROBLEM-SOLVING WORKSHEET

Names _____

_____

_____

The Problem	Ways to Solve the Problem	The Solution

SEQUENCE CHART

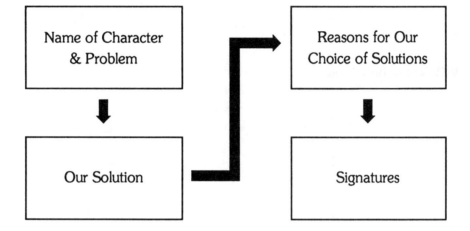

THE HARE AND THE TORTOISE

a. What is the conflict in the story?

b. How was the conflict solved?

c. Who had the best solution? (Each student give at least one reason.)

1.

2.

3.

BULLY UP WORKSHEET

a. What do you think the conflict was in this video?
   Conflict:

b. How does it feel to be pushed around by a bully?
   Feelings:

c. What do you think are better ways to deal with a bully?
   Better Ways:

d. Make a play to show one way to deal with a bully other than fighting.
   Agree on why you think this is a better way than fighting.
   Because:

VIDEOS

UNIT 2: **FRIENDSHIP**
Lesson 1: "Making Friends"   "The Lion and the Mouse"

UNIT 4: **WORKING TOGETHER**
Lesson 2: "Cooperation at the Circus"   "Circus!"

UNIT 5: **PROBLEM SOLVING**
Lesson 1: "What's the Problem?"   "Nate the Great and the Sticky Case"

Lesson 5: "Problem-Solving Stories"   "The Tinder Box"
                                          "The Emperor's New Clothes"
                                          "The Staunch Tin Soldier"
                                          "Sleeping Beauty"
                                          "Little Tom Thumb"
                                          "The Frog Prince"
                                          "Tale of the Ugly Duckling"
                                          "Hansel and Gretel"
                                          "Rumplestiltskin"
                                          "The Boy Who Cried Wolf"
                                          "The Ears of King Midas"

UNIT 6: **CONFLICT RESOLUTION**
Lesson 3: "Hare and Tortoise"   "The Hare and the Tortoise"

Lesson 4: "Bully Up"   "Bully Up: Fighting Feelings"

Contact: Encyclopaedia Britannica Educational Corporation
            Attn: Customer Service
            Britannica Center
            310 S. Michigan Avenue
            Chicago, IL 60604
            1-800-554-9862 or 1-312-347-7900 ext. 6566

REFERENCES

Bellanca, J. and Fogarty, R. *Blueprints for Thinking in the Cooperative Classroom*. Skylight Publishing, Palatine, Illinois, 1990.

Borba, M. and Borba, C. *Self-Esteem: A Classroom Affair* (vol. 1 and 2). Harper and Row, San Francisco, California, 1978.

Canfield, J. and Wells, H.C. *100 Ways to Enhance Self-Concept in the Classroom*. Prentice-Hall, Englewood Cliffs, New Jersey, 1976.

Chase, L. *The Other Side of the Report Card*. Scott Foresman, Glenview, Illinois, 1975.

Chihak, M. and Heron, B. *Games Children Should Play*. Scott Foresman, Glenview, Illinois, 1980.

Cohen, E. *Designing Groupwork: Strategies for the Heterogeneous Classroom*. Teachers College Press, New York, 1986.

Comer, J. "Making Schools Work for Underachieving Minority Students." Paper from a conference entitled *Our National Dilemma*, 1987.

Crary, E. *Kids Can Cooperate*. Parenting Press, Seattle, Washington, 1984.

Curran, L. and Kagan, S. *Cooperative Learning Lessons for Little Ones*. Resources for Teachers, San Juan Capistrano, California, 1991.

Deutsch, M. "An Experimental Study of the Effects of Cooperation and Competition Upon Group Processes." *Human Relations*. Vol. 2, 1949.

Fogarty, R. and Opeka, K. *Start Them Thinking*. Skylight Publishing, Palatine, Illinois, 1988.

Gibbs, J. *Tribes*. Center Source Publications, Santa Rosa, California, 1987.

Glasser, W. *Control Theory in the Classroom*. Harper & Row, New York, 1986.

Johnson, D. and Johnson, R. *Leading The Cooperative School*. Interaction Book Company, Edina, Minnesota, 1989.

Johnson, D.; Johnson, R.; Johnson-Holubec, E. *Circles of Learning*. Interaction Book Company, Medina, Minnesota, 1990.

Joyce, B.; Showers, B.; Rolheiser-Bennett, C. "Staff Development and Student Learning: A Synthesis of Research on Models of Teaching." *Educational Leadership*, Vol. 45, No. 2, October, 1987.

Kagan, S. "Social Motives and Behaviors of Mexican American and Anglo American Children," *Chicano Psychology*. Academic Press, New York, 1977.

Kohn, A. *No Contest: The Case Against Competition*. Houghton-Mifflin, Boston, 1986.

Marcus, S.A. and Bellanca, J. *Early Stars*. Skylight Publishing, Palatine, Illinois, 1988.

Marcus, S.A. and McDonald, P. *Tools For The Cooperative Classroom*. Skylight Publishing, Palatine, Illinois, 1990.

McCabe, M. and Rhoades, J. *The Nurturing Classroom*. ITA Publications, Willits, California, 1988.

Michaelis, B. and Michaelis, D. *Learning Through Noncompetitive Activities and Play*. Education Today Company, Inc., Palo Alto, California, 1977.

Oakes, J. and Lipton, M. *Making the Best of Schools*. Yale University Press, New Haven, 1990.

Opeka, K. *Keep Them Thinking, Level I*. Skylight Publishing, Palatine, Illinois, 1989.

Orlick, T. *Cooperative Sports and Games* (Vol. I and II). Pantheon Books, New York, 1982.

Sharan, S. and Sharan, Y. *Small-Group Teaching*. Educational Technology Publications, Englewood Cliffs, New Jersey, 1976.

Slavin, R.E. *Cooperative Learning*. Longman, New York, 1983.

Stone, J. and Kagan, S. *Cooperative Learning and Language Arts*. Resources for Teachers, San Juan Capistrano, California, 1989.

Weinstein, M. and Goodman, J. *Playfair: Everybody's Guide to Non-Competitive Play*. Impact Publishers, San Luis Obispo, California, 1980.

Additional resources to increase your teaching expertise...

1

SKYLIGHT PUBLISHING, INC.

The Skylight Catalog

The Skylight Catalog presents a selection of the best publications from nationally recognized authorities on **cooperative learning, thinking, whole language, self-esteem, substance abuse prevention, multiple intelligences,** and **school restructuring.**

2

The **IRI** Group

Training

IRI training is available through inservices, seminars, and conferences. Participants gain practical techniques and strategies for implementing the latest findings from educational research. IRI training provides necessary educational skills at a cost educators can afford.

3

The **IRI** Group

Training of Trainers

IRI provides inservice training for experienced educators who are designated to train other staff members. The training of trainers provides techniques for effectively introducing the latest strategies to peer educators.

**To receive a free copy of the
Skylight Catalog, or for more information about
trainings offered by IRI, contact:**

IRI/Skylight Publishing, Inc.
200 E. Wood Street, Suite 250, Palatine, Illinois 60067
Toll free 800-348-4474
(In northern Illinois 708-991-6300) FAX 708-991-6420

There are
one-story intellects,
two-story intellects, and three-story
intellects with skylights. All fact collectors who have
no aim beyond their facts are one-story men. Two-story men compare,
reason, generalize, using the labor of fact collectors as their own.
Three-story men idealize, imagine, predict—
their best illumination comes
from above the skylight.
—*Oliver Wendell*
Holmes